ROUTING
FOR BEGINNERS

SECOND REVISED AND EXPANDED EDITION

ANTHONY BAILEY

ROUTING
FOR BEGINNERS

SECOND REVISED AND EXPANDED EDITION

This edition published 2012 by
Guild of Master Craftsman Publications Ltd
Castle Place, 166 High Street, Lewes,
East Sussex BN7 1XU

First edition published 1999 (ISBN 978-1-86108-101-8)
First revised and expanded edition published 2004 (ISBN 978-1-86108-318-0)

Publisher Jonathan Bailey
Production Manager Jim Bulley
Managing Editor Gerrie Purcell
Senior Project Editor Virginia Brehaut
Copy Editor Nicola Hodgson
Managing Art Editor Gilda Pacitti
Design Rob Janes

Set in Futura and Aachen
Colour origination by GMC Reprographics
Printed and bound in China by Hing Yip Printing Co. Ltd

*To my wife Patsy, and my family Alex,
Lucy, Amber and Francis, not forgetting
the guinea pigs Colban and Polo and
Charlie the dog – they all make my life
quite special.*

CONTENTS

Projects for the home 177

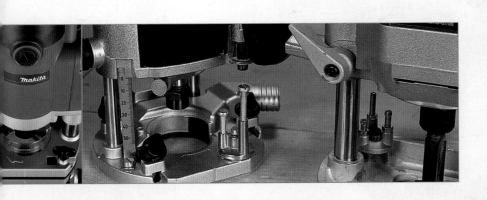

INTRODUCTION

The original edition of this book was published in 1999, so it is no wonder that I have been asked to update it. Looking back at the previous revised and expanded edition made me realize how much has changed; things don't stand still in the world of routing any more than they do in the rest of human activity. A number of models or types of router have disappeared, been replaced, or even reintroduced. There has been a consolidation of brands in the marketplace, which could limit a buyer's choice, although there are still plenty of router models out there to choose from.

What is it about a router that makes it so special? It is, of course, its versatility: no other power tool can do all the things a router can. Routers are highly portable, so you have the means to work both on-site and in the workshop, and to carry out all manner of operations. Moulding, jointing, trimming, drilling – you name it, the router can probably do it.

I have written a companion volume to this one entitled *Router Jigs and Templates*, in which I stress the need for flexibility with control. If there is one major lesson to learn in using a router, it is how to make it do exactly what you want. I hope you will find useful advice within these pages, not just how to master the basics, but also about how to avoid the perils and pitfalls that can occur if you do not fully understand the principles of machining with a router.

All of us woodworkers engage in this activity, whether as a hobby or for work, because we enjoy using our practical skills to produce real, useful results. It follows that we need to do so safely and in a pleasant working environment.

I hope you enjoy reading this book as much as I have enjoyed writing it, and that you can take advice and inspiration from it to expand your experience of working with routers.

Happy reading.

Anthony Bailey

■ A NOTE ABOUT CONVERSIONS

This book was written in the UK, and I think we can be proud of our ability to compromise and 'fudge' important matters so they suit us. Unfortunately, this also extends to measurements; we buy kitchen units as 1,000mm-long metric bases, but we drive on roads measured in miles. We buy sugar by the kilo, but fruit in pounds, and so it goes on. Where woodworking is concerned – and routing in particular – this occurs all the time. Manufactured boards in the UK are sold in metric thickness;

softwoods are sold by the metre run, whereas hardwoods, irrespective of the imported sizes, are usually sold by the cubic foot, which is a much more manageable size than a cubic metre.

In the UK, router cutter shanks and collets run: ¼in, 8mm and ½in; in Europe, they run in 6mm and 12mm. However, ¼in and ½in cutters are referred to as 6.35mm and 12.7mm respectively because they are part of a series of metric sizes sold by

manufacturers and these two are traditional preferred sizes with users. So the cutter on the front end is in metric, while the same size shank at the back end is imperial, strictly speaking...

We Brits deal with this all the time and I'm sure the engineers among the readership will work this all out easily. For everyone else, I hope you can make the necessary leaps of thinking required, although I don't think it will be a major problem.

GETTING STARTED

CHAPTER 1

INTRODUCING THE ROUTER

The router is a jack of all trades and a master of all of them.
A router can tackle all of the following woodworking tasks, and
many more, with ease. Whether in the workshop or on site, there is
no other power tool as versatile or as capable as a router. Provided
you have a good selection of cutters to suit your needs, the router can
perform various tricks and make all sorts of machining possible that
could otherwise only be done with large stationary machines such as
the spindle moulder or chisel mortiser.

The once great name in routing – ¼in Trend T5 going at full blast.

Creating tiny mouldings for a dolls' house.

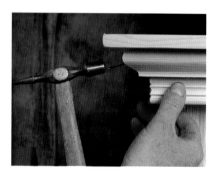

Making full-sized cornices and handrailing.

Rebating, grooving and dovetailing.

Making mortise-and-tenon joints.

Biscuit jointing.

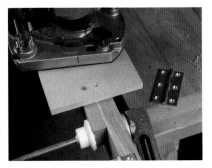
Tongue-and-grooving repetitive shape cutting with templates, for example for locks or hinges.

Edge-planing boards.

Cutting post-form kitchen worktop joints.

Levelling the groundwork for relief carving.

Precision-drilling hinge and shelf support holes.

Producing raised and fielded panels and door frames.

Carving a name on a signboard.

Trimming laminates.

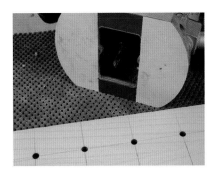
Drilling holes.

WHAT IS A ROUTER?

You may occasionally come across an old-fashioned hand router in a second-hand toolshop. Apart from the name, this tool bears little resemblance to the subject of this book. A hand router was used to fashion slots or housings in wood – a job it did reasonably well for a long time. It shares this ability with the portable electric router, but that is about all the two tools have in common. Hand routers are still available, as there has been a recent resurgence of interest in new, high-quality hand tools.

The modern router is descended from fixed-head machines; these are still used in industry today, although usually under computer control. Once this machine grew legs (or plunge columns, to be more precise) and walked, it became a wholly different animal in machining terms. A router has a motor and a switchgear, a base to keep it stable and perpendicular to the work surface, handgrips to keep it under control, and a means of pushing the cutter into the work (plunging). It features a plunge lock and a depth stop to give a precise depth of cut, and a fence for guiding the router cutter along the side of a workpiece. Fixed-base routers (see p. 21) have a means of screw height adjustment and need to be lowered onto the work while running or entered from the end or side into the work. That, in essence, is all there is to the router.

An old wooden hand router. The original owner's name is stamped on both ends.

ROUTER HISTORY

The first handheld router was a monstrous machine that was designed for routing stair strings (the boards at the sides of a staircase that the treads and risers fit into). This router was supposedly invented in 1906 and sold by Stevenson Machine Co., which went on to become the Kelley Electric Machine Co. This company survived until about 1920. The patent for this machine is dated 28 January 1908, by George L. Kelley of Buffalo, NY (New York). It had two spindles that accepted two cutting bits at the same time. The Kelley Router was at least twice the size of a comparable router today. However, the bits rotated at a mere 6,500rpm (more akin to a static spindle moulder).

A Stanley-Carter router.

The first patent for a single spindle router like today's machines was given to Ray L. Carter who set up a company in Phoenix, NY called R. L. Carter Co., which he later sold to The Stanley Works in 1929. Most woodworkers will be familiar with Stanley Tools who are still going strong but no longer manufacture routers themselves.

The first plunge router, as opposed to the fixed-base type, was introduced in Germany in 1949 by ELU (named after the founder of the company Eugen Lutz). Most but not all modern routers are plunge type, but sadly ELU power tools are no longer made as this division of the company was bought by Black & Decker Group who in turn have merged with Stanley Works.

THE STRENGTHS OF A ROUTER

An ordinary mains-powered drill has a top speed of about 3,500rpm (revolutions per minute), whereas the router has a top speed of between 18,000rpm and 25,000rpm (depending on the size of the machine). This massive increase in speed is achieved by the router's higher level of efficiency. Because router cutters have a small diameter, this equates well with the average industrial spindle moulder running at only 6,000rpm, but compensated by much bigger cutter blocks (4–6in/10–15cm in diameter or even larger) and a considerable hike in kinetic energy.

The router has to achieve tremendous power with much smaller, less efficient means at its disposal. Its solution is to drastically increase speed at the edge of the cutter; hence the high motor speed. At this kind of rpm, the cutter will attack the work, slicing into the wood with an efficiency and smoothness that could not be managed at a much lower speed. At a lower speed, the result would be very rough and ragged, and the machine would proceed at a very uneven feed rate, leaving a messy trail and severe burn marks where the cutter passes over the wood. It would also cause the cutter to become overheated and dangerously damaged, and the motor would likely burn out quickly. Last of all, a slow machine could not manage anything like the size or depth of cut achievable with a high-speed motor.

It follows that anything that challenges the forces of nature so severely in terms of mass, momentum and friction also challenges the technology that creates it. Indeed, although current machines are pretty reliable, the history of the router is peppered with failed machines and cutters that just could not take the strain. Such a dynamic piece of equipment needs to be harnessed so that it can be used safely and successfully.

A heavily built, well-guarded Rojek spindle moulder.

CONTROL OF THE ROUTER

The router is potentially a very accurate way to perform all kinds of machining operations. However, if you just use it straight out of the box in its most basic freehand mode then you may sometimes be disappointed. It can run cutters at high speed so they can machine with precision but the movement of the router, the direction it moves in and how that movement is controlled will determine how accurate the result will be. The standard straight fence works reasonably well but there are plenty of occasions where it simply cannot deliver the right result. An example is where you want to machine at the beginning and end of an edge as well as all the way in between. The middle section is no problem but there isn't enough support for the fence and the router base at the start and finish. The simplest answer is to clamp a batten alongside that oversails the ends; this gives the extra support required.

So as you go along learning how to use the router, consider ways in which you can keep it on track and doing what you want it to do. When you have worked through all the chapters in this book and tried your hand at various techniques and projects you may want to go to the next stage and read the companion volume to this one entitled *Router Jigs and Templates*, which shows more advanced ways to tame your machine.

TYPES OF ROUTER

Routers come in two basic types: either plunge-body or fixed-base models. Most routers in Europe are the plunge-body type but more recently fixed-base models, which are popular in the USA, have made a comeback, usually as part of a swap-body kit, where one motor can fit either base.

Whereas vision of the cutting area when using a plunge machine is good, fixed bases tend to offer less vision of what is happening. Plunging allows you to enter the workpiece at any point, whereas the fixed-base type can only be entered from the side or end of a workpiece. One good reason for having a swap-body model is to keep the fixed base mounted in a router table for rapid changeover. However, either type can be used inverted in a table.

A typical fixed-base router.

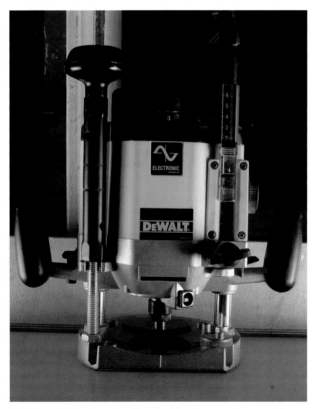

A table-mounted router can be either a fixed-base type or a plunge model, as shown here.

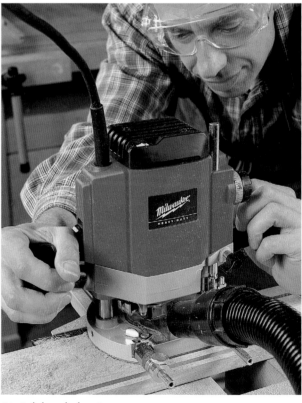

A typical plunge-body router.

THE PLUNGE-BODY ROUTER

The photograph below shows the internal and external features of a modern DeWalt plunge-body router. Basic routers come in a number of sizes, such as ¼in, ⅜in and ½in (this size refers to maximum collet capacities). Not all routers have inbuilt extraction, which is a pity as it ensures that extraction is always possible when routing; however, it does restrict vision of the work area somewhat.

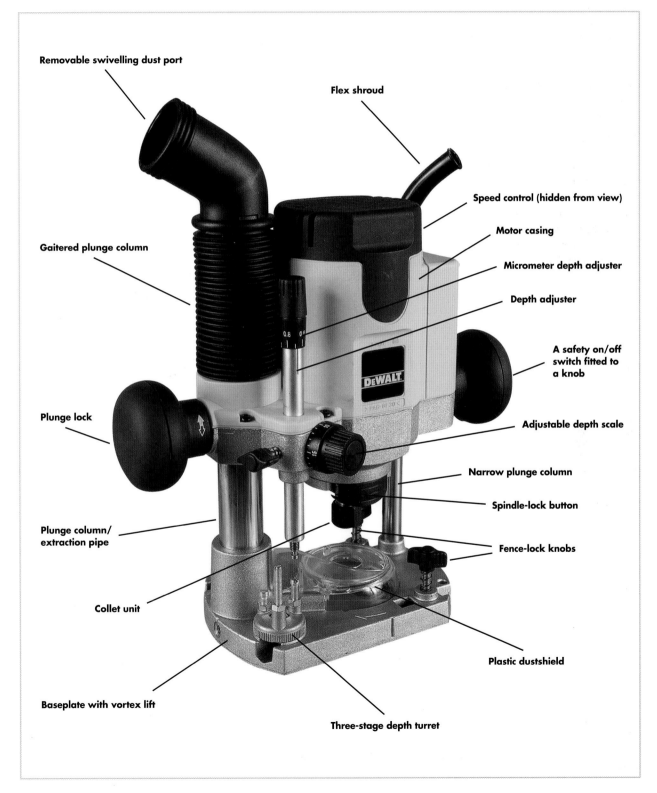

Removable swivelling dust port

Flex shroud

Speed control (hidden from view)

Motor casing

Gaitered plunge column

Micrometer depth adjuster

Depth adjuster

A safety on/off switch fitted to a knob

Plunge lock

Adjustable depth scale

Narrow plunge column

Spindle-lock button

Plunge column/ extraction pipe

Fence-lock knobs

Collet unit

Plastic dustshield

Baseplate with vortex lift

Three-stage depth turret

THE MAIN PARTS OF A ROUTER

Familiarizing yourself with the main parts of your router will really help you enormously when you first start woodworking with this useful machine. See also pp. 24–25; 'Learning to use your router'.

The motor

Routers work at high speeds and the cutters are put under a lot of strain, so it is important that the motor is well balanced. The weight of the motor core must be evenly distributed to give a smooth and reasonably quiet motor that will have a long service life. If this part goes wrong, machine failure is guaranteed. Simpler motors have just a few windings, but the router has a multi-wound motor for even and continuous performance. The motor sits inside an outer series of windings, which create a magnetic effect opposite to that produced in the motor core's own windings; the result is very rapid production of a high rotational speed. This quick build-up to running speed, coupled with the heavy forces applied to the cutter under load, means that special high-speed bearings are required.

These are usually sealed to keep out dust and resin, which would soon gum up the ballraces and grind them down, thus creating loose, dry, overheated bearings. There is also a sealed long-life switch. Together, these are the items that make a router 'go'.

Electronics package

Most routers carry an electronics package that enables them to start gently rather than in a sudden, unnerving jumpstart that can pull a large router out of your hands. Another advantage of the electronics package is the matching of motor power to load: the heavier the cut, the more power courses through the motor. This explains the higher wattage of electronic models: they need more power for the electronics to work, but mainly to allow the motor to apply extra power so that it can operate at a constant speed, whatever the demands placed upon it. A choice of speeds allows the use of high speeds for small-diameter cutters and low speeds for large cutters or special materials such as hard plastics. Bearings and switches are common fail points, but

these are replaceable, providing the fault is divined quickly enough (see Chapters 2 and 3 for more on repairs and maintenance).

Collets and cutters

The cutters are fitted to the lower end of the motor shaft via a collet. Collets differ from drill chucks in that the collet is a precision-milled split sleeve designed to hold cutters of just one shank size, whereas a chuck has movable jaws to grip drills of different sizes. A chuck works well enough in a slow-speed drill, but for precision high-speed work the collet is the only practical solution (except for industrial cutters that are screwed directly onto the shaft). Normally a router will take different-sized collets, allowing a variety of cutters to be used. A retaining nut holds and clamps the collet tightly, thus gripping the cutter shank tightly. Special care must be taken with all collets to ensure that no damage results either to them or to the cutters (see p. 24). A combination of spanner and shaft lock, or two spanners, allows the collet to be tightened or loosened for inserting or removing cutters.

Top row: L-R ½in and ¼in collet extenders, two ¼in collet inserts, two small ¼in collets. Middle row: L-R ¼in, 8mm, 10mm, ½in collets and ½in collet mounted in nut, all designed to fit in a ½in router. Bottom row: L-R Bosch 8mm and ½in collets, ¼in DeWalt collet, ditto mounted in nut, Trend T5 8mm collet in nut.

Plunge mechanism

For plunging to work, the router needs two smooth, machined columns fixed to the base. The body slides up and down these with one, or very rarely, two phosphor bronze sleeves inside the motor housing acting as slide bearings. Occasional lubrication is required to keep the plunge action smooth. On one column a lever or knob acts to lock it at the required height and must not slip due to machining effort or vibration. When locked the motor body should be rigid and there should be very little play when it is unlocked.

Fixed-body mechanism

Usually the motor can slide into the fixed base engaging in either a toothed track or a gradient track in the casting. This allows controlled raising and lowering of the motor. A latch or lock of some kind is used to fix the correct cutting height. The sliding action up and down should be very smooth and not require lubrication, which would be messy. If the router is a swap-body model the mechanisms may be slightly different to separates-only machines.

These two compact routers demonstrate the difference between a plunge model on the left and fixed-base on the right.

Plunging

Plunge-type routers have two very rigid, well-machined columns on which the body is mounted. To operate them, you undo the plunge lock and push the body down, against spring pressure. Then you engage the lock once more at full-plunge depth (this depth depends on what setting you have made). The plunge lock can consist of either a twist handgrip or an entirely separate lever at the back of the machine. It is normal to machine in several passes so as not to strain either the motor or the cutter; therefore an adjustable depth stop and a three-stage revolving turret are fitted on all machines. This allows quick resetting between passes so that the final depth is reached in safe stages. The depth-setting rod may be very simple, with nothing more than a lock knob to hold it, or it may be a more precise geared rise-and-fall type.

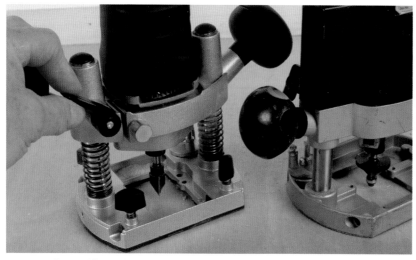

Two routers showing different plunge locks.

A geared rise-and-fall depth rod and turret stop.

The base

The base is as important as any other part of a router; the motor must sit squarely upon it, without being at all unstable, and it must keep the cutter exactly perpendicular to the work surface. The hole in the base needs to be able to admit any size cutter within the designed capacity of that machine. However, the base is more than just a support: it will take guide bushes for when you want to cut around templates; it has holes for the supporting rods for the fence, and to take a roller guide and trammel bar for circle cutting; it has table-mounting holes, and it may accept a guide rail.

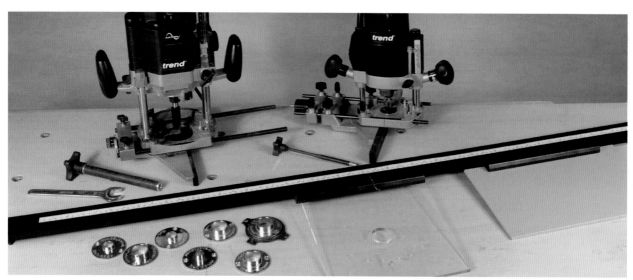

Both large and small routers accept these accessories.

Dust extraction

Some routers have built-in extraction for dust and chippings rather than the usual bolt-on facility. Extraction facilities tend to obscure the work and are inconvenient, but self-preservation makes extraction with a machine as messy as the router an absolute must.

The Makita RPC1110C has extraction built into the base with a removable external extraction pipe; the fence has an extraction bowl as well.

THE FIXED-BASE ROUTER

The fixed-base router (also called a swap-body router) is the other main type of router. It was once largely a product of the USA and had all but disappeared from the UK and the rest of Europe. After a long period of absence, however, there are now several models available in the UK, including ones from DeWalt and Bosch. These are also available as twin-base models, which give you the best of both worlds – that is they provide an interchangeable plunge and fixed bases.

There are merits to this type of router, which neatly combines depth-of-cut adjustment with the actual height setting. There is no swift plunging action here – you carefully lower the router into the work. Plunging is not perfect: the plunge action is not always silky-smooth and can result in a slight divot where the plunge is first made. The fixed-base router, with its wide overall base size and lack of 'bounceback', is in some ways more predictable. You can also slide the machine into the work, for instance when cutting a through slot.

A Draper professional twin-base router fitted with an LED worklight and complete with all its supplied accessories, including guide bushes, roller guide and dust spouts.

DIFFERENT SIZES OF ROUTER

Apart from the very smallest machines, it is not always easy to tell what power each machine is. The key place to look is the specification plate or label, which indicates the wattage. Another clue is the range of collets that are available for each router.

Lightweight routers

The smallest router is probably the 'palm grip' router, which has about 600 watts of motor power for smaller work and only a ¼in collet. Then there is a larger professional type with 720 watts minimum, or, in the case of the DeWalt 621E, a great 1,100 watts of power. Bosch makes 1,200- and 1,400-watt models. This size of router can usually take ¼in and 8mm collets. Cheaper routers have collets that tend to be simpler and smaller than those supplied with the professional models, and the kit comes with other bits and pieces so that you can start working immediately.

The professional models have everything built on a much heavier scale; the collets are better made and come in a wider range of sizes. All of the attachments are larger and you will need to buy them separately. These machines are designed for precision working; fine adjusters are available, as are a variety of guide bushes and a router table. These machines are capable of repetitive and quite punishing work in a professional environment.

The size difference is obvious here. The Bosch boasts compactness, which suits many purposes; at the other extreme, the ½in Hitachi has a heavily overbuilt casing to make it look more impressive. The ¼in Trend T5 in the middle is a more typical machine in terms of size and power. Note that the term '¼in router' usually ignores the fact that a larger 8mm collet can also be fitted.

Medium-duty routers

Medium-duty models have made a comeback recently. They offer a power rating combined with a ½in collet size that is useful where a really big machine is not required.

Heavy-duty routers

The ½in router is no longer only for professionals. These models are very heavily built and come with a choice of collets or collet inserts (see p. 50 on cutter safety). A straight fence is standard, but all accessories are extras. Its power and size mean that this type of machine will handle any task with ease. Models with motor wattages of around 1,600–2,000 are made, although 1,700–1,850 is a typical rating. Electronics are essential for maintaining the right speed with any size cutter, as these machines will work with both tiny and huge cutters. The best models are as accurate to use as a ¼in router, but some can be a bit rough and ready in their adjustments.

■ EXTRACTION SYSTEMS

Extraction on routers is a contentious issue. It is a must, but manufacturers need to work much harder at finding convenient solutions. Virtually all machines, in all categories, can take an extraction pipe as an extra, although more machines now have an in-built extraction system, usually with a vortex lift to encourage dust to move quickly out of the machining area. They sometimes also have an extraction bowl fitted to the fence for edge working. These days, there is no excuse for other machines not to have this kind of built-in facility.

The base of the DeWalt 621E, showing the vortex design extraction system.

The popular palm router ('grip' router would be a more accurate description), which, although not marketed as such, can be used as a laminate trimmer.

SPECIALIST ROUTERS

The laminate trimmer can be a handy little machine. It has quite a small 'footprint', tending to be taller than it is wide. You may wish to use a fence or roller guide with it, although it is more usual to use bearing-guided cutters. Generally these will be bevel or chamfer cutters, though any small profile could be used if you are working on materials other than laminates. These machines usually have around 600 watts of power, which is quite a lot. For many purposes, this machine could prove handy as an alternative to a professional ¼in router.

There are several machines on the market designed for tasks such as cleaning putty from glazing rebates or for machining aluminium sections. They are made with double-glazing manufacturers in mind, so are not really of interest outside their target market.

LEARNING TO USE YOUR ROUTER

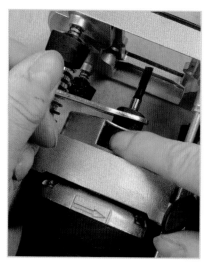

1 When you take your new router out of the box, first read the manufacturer's instructions and understand them – it might make a significant difference. Ensure that there are no loose parts, especially any that might have become lodged in the machine itself and pose a hazard when it is switched on. The machine used in this step-by-step sequence is the well-established Trend T4. The depth stop, scale and turret are at the front, and the router is at rest and unplunged. The motor, and therefore any cutter that might be fitted, is well clear of the workpiece.

2 Make sure that your router is unplugged and then lay it down so that you can fit the cutter. Some models have a flat-topped motor housing and can be rested on this. The Trend T4, like most routers, has a spindle-lock button that is very convenient. Select a small, two-flute, straight cutter for making this experimental cut. Usually a new router will be supplied with one, and all basic cutter sets include a straight cutter. When fitting a cutter in a collet, make sure there is always at least ¾in (19mm) of cutter in the collet. When you tighten the collet nut it may appear to be gripping, but continue to turn it until it retightens; this is needed as the collet moves into place around the shank. Never overtighten the collet nut – it should be enough to grip the cutter firmly without any risk of the cutter coming out. If you need the strength of a gorilla to undo the collet nut, you have probably tightened it too much!

3 Set the electronic speed control to match the cutter you have just fitted. If this is left until later, you might forget and start cutting without having made the adjustment. In general terms, a small cutter should be run faster than a large cutter, so in this case, top speed will be fine. (Chapters 3 and 4 provide further useful information on selecting cutting speeds.)

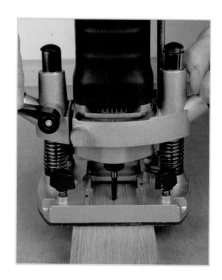

4 With the power still off, gently plunge the stationary cutter until it just touches the workpiece. Push the plunge-lock lever to the 'on' position; the motor head then stays in this place. The workpiece must be clamped down before carrying out this operation.

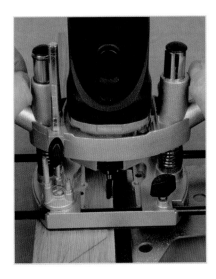

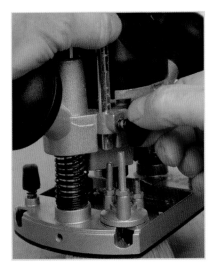

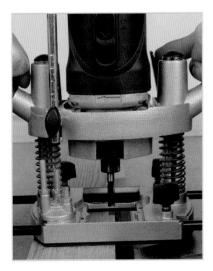

5 Decide how deep you will need to plunge. A guideline is that the cut depth should not be greater than the diameter of the cutter shank: about ¼–⁹⁄₃₂in (6–7mm) per pass is safe (see step 4). Move the depth rod up or down until the gap between it and the stop on the base is about ¼–⁹⁄₃₂in (6–7mm). You can check this measurement by using a ruler or even a metric drill-bit with a shank of the right diameter. If you want to make a deeper cut in two passes, the two milled nuts on the rod can be turned to set an upper and lower limit. Then, after the first pass, press the sprung button and push the rod up to the top setting, ready for the second pass. This does not allow for a situation where, for instance, very deep cutting is being done with a ½in shank cutter on a large router. In this case, professionals often make each pass, setting the depth by eye, using the turret setting for the last pass only. This is not recommended if you are new to routing. You need to learn how to machine safely, and not all cutter and machine combinations behave in the same way. (See Chapter 3 for more information on router safety.)

6 Fit the router side fence and lock it in place with the knobs on the base. The intended test workpiece must be clamped down for safety. Failure to do this will end in disaster – a minor one, maybe, but a disaster nonetheless. Before starting a cut, it is vital to recognize which direction you should be cutting in. When machining an edge rather than the centre of a workpiece, the direction that the cutter is fed into the work should be against the rotation of the cutter. Most routers have an arrow marked on the base to make this obvious. If a cut is made in the wrong direction, this is known as 'climb cutting' and can result in a rather spectacular 'jump' as the machine is pulled by the cutter along the workpiece. It does this because the cutter acts like a wheel on a car pulling the vehicle along. In this instance, there are sharp blades instead of wheels. The results may not be very serious most of the time, but it is as well to avoid this happening. Cutting in the correct direction means the sharp edge of the cutter is being fed into the workpiece.

7 On the workpiece, hold the router in position with the fence against the edge. With the turret adjusted on to the highest stage for the first cut, switch on, plunge, lock and pull the router towards you, taking care to keep the fence against the workpiece. Stop cutting after say 12in (30cm), release the plunge lock so the cutter can spring back out of the work, and switch off. That is your first cut, and is very easy to make. However, there is more to routing than that. The succeeding chapters will show you the many virtues of this effortlessly versatile machine.

★ **WORKING TIP**

If you are a newcomer to routing it can be rather alarming working out the basics. Remember to make sure you have tightened the cutter enough, without over-tightening, and always cut into the direction the cutter is rotating. Lastly, always unplug between cutter changes. Observe these basic rules and you will stay safe.

CHAPTER 2

CHOOSING A ROUTER

There is a profusion of routers on the market today, from virtually every power-tool manufacturer in the world. This chapter sets out to help you through the confusion that can surround difficult purchasing decisions.

PICKING THE RIGHT ROUTER

There are always awkward choices to be made when we have to buy anything new. Money is often the deciding factor, although on examination of my past buying habits I realize that considerations of quality, reliability and extendibility also played a large part. I have also learned from experience that you do get what you pay for. A cheap piece of equipment cannot realistically be expected to match the performance of an expensive one, or even to keep on working – there are a few exceptions, but not many, so bear this in mind when looking for a router.

Believe it or not, this very substantial piece of furniture intended to be a media centre for a flat-screen television (see pp. 204–217) can be made entirely using a standard ¼in router. You don't necessarily need a large router for large pieces of work!

Making a list of your requirements will help, because it narrows the field considerably. Reading about tests in woodworking magazines and fielding the opinions and experiences of fellow woodworkers may also be useful, not to mention the occasional chance of a 'hands-on' test. Unfortunately, finding and interpreting all this data is difficult, which is where this book comes in.

Bearing in mind that this is a book for those with limited or no experience of routing, the next section (see p. 32), which discusses actual models, covers machines that are readily available rather than the strictly trade-only or the more esoteric machines. Below I outline a number of factors that might influence which router you decide to buy.

ROUTER SIZE AND POWER

Ask yourself honestly: what do I expect to do with this machine? If your aim is to complete a few jobs around the house and create some nice pieces of furniture, then you will not need a top-range German Festool ½in router with a price tag to match. Likewise, if you want to tackle very heavy work – perhaps some joinery such as window sashes or handrailing – then a small, lightweight, do-it-yourself router will not meet your requirements.

So, consider the tasks you have in mind. If this is your first router, it would probably be best to purchase a ¼in model. It will be cheaper, the cutters are smaller (and cheaper), and it isn't a monster to use. In fact, a large percentage of machining can be undertaken with a ¼in router quite successfully with a little ingenuity. Power isn't lacking these days, although multiple passes will be needed to avoid breaking the narrow-shank cutters.

For some tasks the laminate trimmer or palm router is perfectly adequate. If you use a small cutter, the compact footprint of these mini machines is good and you can work on smaller projects such as boxes or even work in situ overhead.

Machining a mortise with a mortise box.

SYSTEM EXTENDIBILITY

Only you know what work you expect to undertake, although once you get to know the machine better, other ways of using it might become apparent. Also, larger projects would benefit from you acquiring a much bigger machine. Planning ahead might entail buying a small router now, with the possibility of acquiring a larger model later. System extendibility plays a part here, because a ¼in router from manufacturer 'X' might have components that will work with their own ½in model, but not with the ½in machine from manufacturer 'Y'.

ERGONOMICS AND GENERAL HANDLING

Ergonomics are important. It is easy to be swayed by the look of a particular router and then find it has uncomfortable handles and knobs, or fiddly controls, such as a speed-setting wheel that is recessed too far into the case and hard to turn. Some simpler routers have stamped-steel plunge levers that some people find unpleasant to operate, especially when they are used to the European models. Some ½in routers are not only big in themselves, but sometimes have very large handgrips and controls that are awkward or a bit basic.

When you pick up a router and put it into action, it should feel pleasant to operate, with all controls and switches conveniently to hand. Actions such as plunging should be very smooth and efficient. Things are not always like this, so try several different models before forming an opinion on what suits you. Incidentally, plunge columns sometimes need a little lubrication before they work perfectly. Another operational annoyance can be a mains lead that is too short – this is not insurmountable, but do you really want to put up with it just because a manufacturer was too mean to fit a longer one?

Plunge-lock levers are often ergonomically shaped like this one.

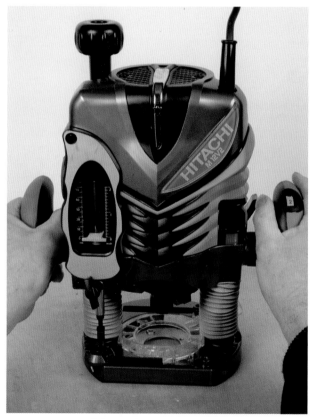

An ergonomic router. All the controls are easy to reach.

KITS AND CASES

Lightweight routers are often sold in kit form, although without a case. The reason for this is that the extra parts are stamped metal and plastic with some standard nuts and bolts. This makes it quite cheap to provide the whole thing in one cardboard box and call it a kit.

The cheaper, less-specified professional models (those with a lower motor rating) may come only with a fence, a dust-spout and a guide bush. This keeps the cost down.

The top-end models, which have electronics and bigger motors, often come in heavy-duty steel cases along with some extras. Usually the 'K' in a model name denotes that it is part of a kit in a case.

It might seem that the first, cheaper option is not such good value, because it comes without extra bits and pieces. However, it may be the right one. You should also consider the price and whether it has a system to back it up. What kind of guide rails, guide bushes and tables go with it? Top-end models are built to a heavier standard and have more power than the cheaper models, because they are aimed at professionals. Take a good look at what rival manufacturers have to offer before making a final decision. However, certain companies, such as Trend Machinery (UK), offer various solutions that will fit a variety of different machines, so it may not be such a problem if your chosen router does not come with all the trimmings.

A typical large router kit, which is supplied in a tough blow-mould case. It contains everything a tradesman needs including a means of guide-bush alignment.

The more recent DeWalt twin-base machine has two of everything: two bases, two fences, two extraction spouts and a blow-mould case to fit it all in.

PRICE VERSUS QUALITY

The power-tool market has changed considerably over the past few years. You can pick up some cheaper routers, often at do-it-yourself superstores, possibly under their own brand name; however, don't expect these models to have a long working life.

When shopping around, you will probably find your local professional shop is quite expensive. Often such shops are selling to trade customers at prices exclusive of VAT, because these customers can reclaim the VAT. The result is that the price sounds reasonable until you add on the tax figure. In fairness, in the course of a year these shops probably won't sell anywhere near as many units as a nationally advertised mail-order outfit, which will normally be selling inclusive of tax, but whose margins can be trimmed to match their larger turnover.

RELIABILITY

We all want something that won't go wrong or give us any trouble. In practice, there is no such guarantee, except the manufacturer's own!

Price does play a part in determining how reliable a router will be. The more expensive machines are a better bet, but even some cheap routers come with extended warranties as standard. As long as a machine is used for the kind of work it was intended for, there should not be too much to worry about.

Regular servicing and prompt repair of worn or damaged parts will do a lot to extend the life of your router. Note the motor brushes and the electronics package, which has been lifted away from the body (see right).

A completely wrecked top bearing, still mounted in the router, compared with an undamaged bottom bearing (held in the hand).

★ WORKING TIP

Cleaning your router will prolong its operating life between having it serviced. The safest way is to use a compressed air-only aerosol or a compressor and nozzle, to blow dust out of the casing. It isn't wise to use oils or spray lubricants except on the plunge rods and the plunge lock.

AVAILABILITY OF SERVICING AND SPARES

Generally speaking, most of the manufacturers that supply the UK market have put in place proper 'spares and repairs' facilities. If you are in doubt before purchasing, check how well the dealer thinks they can cope with any repairs or servicing that you may need.

Most power tools come with an exploded parts diagram. This is important and should be kept safely with the warranty. This means that if a user fit item does go wrong, you can readily identify it. Dealers and service centres need to locate each item on the stock computer, so the exact description and part number are needed. They also need the serial number of the machine. Professionals are often able to have repair work done at short notice. This is only fair, because they need their tools to earn a living; the rest of us may have to wait a bit longer!

Collection of routers ready for routine servicing and maintenance.

■ WARRANTIES AND REPAIRS

Every country has different consumer laws that have to be observed by all power-tool manufacturers and dealers. All tools come with a warranty card that gives details of the warranty terms and conditions as well as details of where to send the tool in the event of failure.

In the UK, amateur equipment is guaranteed for one year. However, professional tools generally have extended warranties and special servicing arrangements that can be particularly attractive to the prospective purchaser. As always, it pays to check what terms are on offer with each tool.

Some professionals do certain repairs themselves, such as changing the switch and bearings. This is not something to be undertaken lightly and should not be attempted by anyone without the relevant knowledge and experience. It can be dangerous to both user and machine (see Chapter 3, p. 44).

ROUTER GALLERY

The following pages show a selection of routers; these represent just a small proportion of all the machines that are being manufactured today in a constantly changing field. Most nominal ¼in routers take 8mm collets as well, while ½in models accept 8mm and ¼in collets.

Black & Decker RP250 10

Bosch 1617EVS

Bosch 1619EVS

Bosch GMF 1400 CE

Bosch GOF 1600 CE

Bosch MRC23EVSK

Bosch POF 1400 and POF 1200AE

DeWalt D26204K

DeWalt DW615

DeWalt DW618D

DeWalt DW625

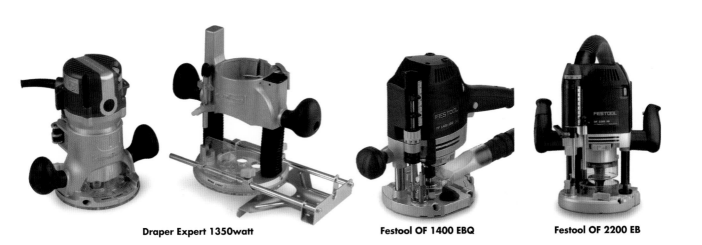

Draper Expert 1350watt

Festool OF 1400 EBQ

Festool OF 2200 EB

Freud FT3000VCE

Hitachi M12V2

Hitachi M12VC

Mafell LO50E

Mafell LO65EC

Makita 3707FC

Makita RD1101

Makita RF1101

Makita RP2301FCX

Milwaukee 5616-20

Porter Cable 450

Porter Cable 7519

Porter Cable 7539   **Skil 1815**   **Skil 1830**

Trend T4   **Trend T5 Mk2**   **Trend T11**

Triton JOF001   **Triton MOF001C**

CHAPTER 3

HEALTH AND SAFETY

My definition of an expert is: 'one who has learned from his or her own mistakes and the mistakes of others'. In other words, if you put into practice the advice in this chapter, you should avoid making some of the errors that I have! Working with tools, whether powered or not, gives plenty of scope for accidents. Common sense, clear thinking and following basic safety rules should mean that the first-aid kit on the workshop wall won't get much use.

ROUTER SAFETY ISSUES

The whole point about safety, which we tend to take for granted, is that it is a series of lessons in how to do the job right and thereby avoid those hideous mistakes that could land us in the emergency room at the hospital. I have had to eat my words before, when I have described a machine as 'relatively safe' and then met someone (sometimes a well-known and respected professional) who has come to grief with that very machine! However, my experiences, and those of other router craftspeople, show that

these machines are pretty safe if used correctly. Nevertheless, that remains the case only if care and common sense keep things that way. It is always a shame to see 'for sale' advertisements in the local paper for items such as 'router and cutters, only used once'. Someone bought a router, tried it and didn't like it. After all, anything whirling quickly with sharp cutting edges can seem forbidding, especially if it manages to mangle wood, or worse. This chapter should help to point out the most obvious

problems in using a router, as well as some of the unexpected ones. Anything directly relating to safety is to be found here, while safety-related issues, such as working freehand or using a router in a table, are dealt with in the relevant chapters later. There are specialist publications from organizations such as the Health and Safety Executive (UK safety body, website: www.hse.gov.uk) and others dealing with safety issues, but this book puts all router-related safety issues into one handy guide.

WORKING AWAY FROM THE WORKSHOP

The router, like any other power tool, doesn't need to be confined to the workshop. It is easy to forget with a versatile yet relatively lightweight tool like this that it is possible to take it to the work. You can easily work outdoors, in the garden or on a patio, or on an area of hard standing.

You can also work indoors, preferably in a room where other building or decoration work is taking place on account of the mess produced by a router. More controlled environments, such as garages and sheds, are discussed later (see pp. 38–39).

Working in the garden

Gardens are often not level, so find an area that is. Working on concrete or paving is best, and it is easier to sweep up afterwards. If yours is a household of children and animals, ensure that they are kept well away from the working area, because both can show an inquisitiveness bordering on the dangerous. My own experience suggests that it is best if they are somewhere else entirely! Once a mistake happens, it can snowball and can to errors of judgement that further affect safety. Professionals may work in noisy workshops, but they don't suffer the interference of outsiders, of any age or species.

Trying to work amid chaos and clutter is not ideal.

The weather is a prime factor to consider when working out of doors; rain and electricity don't mix. Do not be tempted to finish that last cut as the rain begins to fall; it isn't safe, and neither are puddles on the ground where extension cables are lying. You should always plug into an RCD-controlled socket for safety.

Supporting the work

Good work support is essential. Small items will clamp adequately onto the ubiquitous Workmate or similar appliance, but long workpieces or 8 x 4ft (2,440 x 1,220mm) boards need two sawhorses: ready-made ones are available to buy, or you can build your own. See pp. 172–175 for an explanation of how to achieve a low-cost but substantial board-cutting and support set-up.

Dust extraction is essential when working outdoors.

Clearing up

Even though you are working out of doors, it is still worth having dust extraction, otherwise the mess goes everywhere and can be difficult to sweep up. This subject is covered fully in the section on router safety (see pp. 44).

Noise

Noise pollution is a very real hazard to the power-tool user, but the noise can be heard by everyone nearby if you aren't careful. It helps if your neighbours show some tolerance towards the work you are trying to do, but we don't all get on with those around us and the result can be that almost any activity can provoke a negative response. Choosing your time carefully can help. First thing on a Sunday morning is not thoughtful. Likewise, working late at night is not good either, even though the majority of us have to do this work outside of normal hours. By all means ask your neighbours if the noise you are making is acceptable or not, but bear in mind that those who are not making a fuss might just give a polite response when in fact you are disturbing their peace. Working in a workshop or garage can help to deaden sound, depending on how well insulated it is.

When routing outdoors, all you need are a couple of sawhorses and an extension lead.

Just two of a wide variety of work supports that are available on the market.

WORKSHOP SAFETY

A garage or shed is an excellent place in which to carry out woodworking operations. Many of us have one or the other, although they may not be in an appropriate state for immediate use. If you have a proper workshop already, so much the better, but for many this isn't an option and you may only use one occasionally anyway. Below I set out the basic requirements for adapting a garage or shed to be used as a woodworking space.

Repairing the structure

It is well worth the time and effort to repair an existing outbuilding if it is basically sound. Roofs frequently give trouble with leaks, especially flat roofs. If the roofs and gutters are well maintained then the rest of the structure stands a good chance of survival. Windows often leak, but reputtying the glass and replacing rotted sections can give them a new lease of life. Alternatively, you may find some old glazed window units discarded on a building site or at a glass works; these are a cheap (or free) alternative to buying new units, but do ask before you take them. Wooden buildings will benefit from a couple of coats of a good exterior wood finish such as Sikkens or Sadolin, which will seal wood effectively.

Inside the structure, it may be possible to insulate the roof and walls with Rockwool or Celotex insulation board. Lining out with orientated strand board (OSB) or shuttering ply over battens of the existing timber framework will make a more comfortable environment. It is advisable to use builders' quality polythene behind the boarding to keep damp at bay.

A typical garage/workshop.

Applying a new coat of wood protection is a sensible step before the onset of winter.

Power supply

Obviously, you will need a power supply. An extension lead might do temporarily, but a better solution is to install a supply from the house. Consult an electrician about the best way to do this. The choice is between an ordinary cable strung from a tensioned catenary wire between buildings using posts to carry it, or an armoured cable laid underground at the specified depth (usually about 2ft 6in/76cm minimum). An electrician would no doubt be happy for you to dig the trench, but in the UK it is illegal for anyone to connect new works to the mains unless they are qualified to do so. Any electrician who makes that final connection must be qualified to check and certify the whole of the new installation, for which they will make a charge. Do-it-yourself stores sell a lot of electrical materials, such as cables and sockets, but amateur installers should not tackle the work unless they are very experienced and understand the regulations.

One important thing to have is an earth-leakage circuit breaker protecting the entire installation. This may be fitted in the house or in the workshop, depending on the nature of the installation. It means that in an extreme event, such as a circuit fault or lightning strike, the circuit is switched off and made safe. An earth rod will also be required.

Power outlets

If your workshop is an existing building, it may be worth fitting extra power outlets in useful places. Consider using metal-clad sockets, as they are better protected from damage. A ring circuit is needed as it spreads the loading between sockets, but you need to be sure that the installation can cope with the load from a number of sockets.

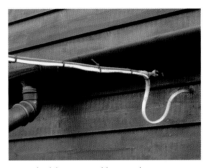

A standard three-core cable strung between two outbuildings from a catenary (suspension cable). Note that the catenary is firmly anchored and the cable hangs in a large drip loop (to avoid water penetrating the building), which also prevents any stress to the copper conductors inside the cable.

Light requirements

You will need good illumination to work by: daylight is ideal, but it should be backed up by an adequate level of artificial light, possibly a mixture of bulbs and fluorescents, because strip lights can be uncomfortable on the eyes. Fitting larger-size windows can help.

Good-size windows plus directional lighting and overhead fluorescent tubes make for a decent light level when working.

Heating the workshop

Care should always be taken with heating any workshop. Electric heaters could overload the circuit, and woodburners may pose a hazard, so think carefully about your particular situation and get advice from friends or professionals. Low-level electrical heating, such as an oil-filled heater that is totally enclosed, often offers the best solution as it can be left on to take the edge off the low temperature, or left on a higher setting with a time-switch so the workshop is warm when you are ready to start routing.

Organizing the space

It is better to work in a building rather than in the open, because it usually contains the noise and you can work despite adverse weather. The downside of being inside is that your working area needs to be large enough and tidy enough to be practical. Aim to

It is relatively easy to put up shelves like these ones fixed to the workshop walls. Size them so you can fit boxes and cases in as well as smaller items, such as the iron used for iron-on veneer tape or the little rebate plane to the right.

create a main area for day-to-day activity while using less-used areas for shelving and cupboards.

The workbench

A workbench of some sort is needed, although it doesn't need to be large. In the age of the power tool, it is more useful to have a solid worksurface away from the walls. This is more suitable for machining operations, whereas a bench needs to be high enough and fitted with a vice to make handwork possible. If you wish to make your own workbench, the board facility (see pp. 172–175) might fit the bill; however, you may wish to make something more substantial with a proper top, even if it is still collapsible. The timber, board and numerous jigs that can proliferate when you work with a router also need to be stored. This may not always be possible, however, so consider buying sheet materials only when you need them.

This is an ideal workbench for working with the router.

■ PURPOSE-BUILT WORKSHOPS

If you have the space and the money, you might consider investing in a purpose-built workshop. Various types are available, but you should be aware of what planning permission may be required. The structure needs to be built on a good sound base such as concrete or timber bearers resting on bricks or blocks to keep it off the damp ground.

Improvements

To make a work area more pleasant may require more drastic measures, especially if you have a bare, dusty, cold concrete floor, such as fitting a plastic damp-proof membrane covered with polyurethane insulation boards and topped off with clip-together flooring chipboard. The result is a warmer, dry, smooth floor that you can even park your car on if it is the garage that gets the treatment.

Reglazing windows with old reclaimed double-glazed units or fitting secondary polycarbonate sheet combined with safe, enclosed (no naked flame or elements) heating can make things much more pleasant in winter.

A purpose-built workshop, good-looking and sturdy, with plenty of storage space in the mansard-type roof.

PERSONAL SAFETY

It is human nature to start a job without getting properly kitted up; we all do it, even, or perhaps especially, professionals. There are a variety of potential risks to the router operator: these may be caused by noise, dust, chippings, loose cutters and broken pieces of cutter material, not to mention accidental abrasion of electrical flex.

All power tools come with a sheet of dos and don'ts, and they are worth reading. Some of these personal warnings are a matter of common sense and simply entail changing the way we approach practical work. Keeping an electrical lead out of harm's way will remove one important risk, while unplugging the router before changing the cutter avoids another. Other safety requirements may entail spending some money and making choices in the process.

Protective clothing and footwear

All woodworking should be done with adequate footwear. I know of several woodworkers who wear sandals; I can only think they must have been lucky not to have dropped something on their feet. Work shoes or boots with reinforcement are best for safety.

Next comes the apron, smock, boiler suit or warehouse coat. You don't have to use proper workwear, but you can at least take it off when you leave the workshop, and it keeps you free from the risk of getting loose clothing caught in the machine. Capacious pockets can be useless, because they can fill with chippings quite quickly. Sleeves should be close-fitting or properly rolled up.

Protection for fingers and hands is covered in Chapter 7 (see p. 102).

Even with good extraction, proper safetywear is essential, particularly to protect the eyes and lungs. However, high-pitched or regular noise levels can cause hearing damage too.

Ear protection

People frequently ignore the need for ear defence. Ear defenders or earplugs are an inconvenience, but they play a vital part in saving your hearing. Routers can have a particularly high-pitched scream, especially when being worked heavily, and continuous exposure to this level of sound can result in loss of hearing at some frequencies and a tendency to acquire tinnitus. The trouble is that ear damage is apparent only after it has already occurred, by which time it is too late – so protect yourself now!

Some people find that earplugs drive dirt and wax back into the ear, in which case ear defenders might be better, because they don't interfere with the workings of the ear. If you use a powered respirator helmet as well, it is necessary to ensure that its headband does not touch that of the ear defenders. This can result in an uncomfortable sound vibration being transmitted from the respirator to your ears, undermining the point of wearing the ear defenders in the first place.

Eye protection

Your eyes are the most immediate safety priority when machining. Being hit in the face by chips of wood or carbide is fairly rare, but it can happen; however, fine dust in your eyes can make them sore and uncomfortable. There is a good variety of safety spectacles available with side shields or ventilated goggles – some of them are quite stylish in appearance. All too often this kind of protection is ignored because it is inconvenient.

Lung protection

It is very important to wear a dust mask or air-fed respirator to protect yourself from dust. The smaller the particles, the more dangerous this dust is. This applies whether it is wood, coal, asbestos or grain dust – it is all very dangerous. Any kind of protection will help, although ordinary 'monkey masks' are less effective and do not last long, so choose the better-quality type instead. Much superior by far, in terms of lung and eye protection, are lightweight air-fed helmets, of

which there are several on the market. These provide clean, filtered air and proper impact protection. The filters last long enough to make them more economical overall, and these helmets are much, much safer than any other product. A small rechargeable battery ensures adequate working time and replaceable visor overlays ensure clear vision. I cannot recommend this kind of protection highly enough; it should be the standard for any woodworker.

Whether you have any breathing problems or not, the most dangerous dust particles aren't the ones you can ordinarily see, they are the sub-micron particles that are less than one micron in size or 1/1,000th of a millimetre. They can penetrate through the skin and into lung tissue because of their minute size, thus potentially causing serious tissue damage. To help counter this, the most effective device is the ambient air filter, available in different sizes to suit most workshops, although these do not necessarily remove the finest particles, they do generally clean the atmosphere. Assuming you have the aforementioned extraction and air cleaning in place, you can then opt for fairly comfortable lightweight personal protection.

This is a typical full-face air-fed respirator helmet. It guarantees pure breathable air using a battery-driven motor and twin microfine air filters. It offers good impact resistance, replaceable visor overlays and add-on ear defenders.

ROUTER SAFETY

If you have spent good money on a new router, you should treat it as your pride and joy and, being new, it should respond in kind. There are a number of safety checks you should carry out before using a router, and if you get into a routine of doing this regularly, your router should give you extended good service.

Checking the plug

Before starting work, there are certain things worth checking for your safety. If a plug is broken or wires are loose, deal with them straightaway. Most new machines come with moulded-on plugs, but if one of these plugs does need replacing, cut the flex close to the plug with wire cutters and dispose of the old plug carefully – it can still be plugged in and has exposed wires that could be lethal (you should remove the wires from a conventional plug completely). Always fit modern plugs of the sturdy rubber sort, with half-sleeved pins (a UK legal requirement), and make sure that you fit a 13-amp fuse.

Checking the lead

The lead should be in good condition, too. Abrasions or cuts can happen quite easily. Also, you should never use the lead as a means of picking up the tool. You might not pull the cable out of the cable grip on the machine, but the copper cores can snap, causing an intermittent on/off effect, which could be dangerous. Replace a faulty lead immediately. Reuse the rubber protector sleeve fitted at the machine end of the lead, because it reduces stress on the lead. You could take the opportunity to fit a longer lead if the original is rather short; anywhere between 8 and 13 ft (2.5–4m) is acceptable. Only do this work if you are confident you understand how to rewire it safely.

Checking for chippings

If the router has been used for inverted machining, check that the casing is free of chippings; it can get packed with them while operating upside-down. The result can be flying debris or a machine that jams when you start it up, but worst of all, the motor windings can get abraded, which may cause the motor to burn out, possibly in spectacular fashion.

Fence-locking knobs

Ensure that fence-locking knobs have anti-vibration springs so that they don't work loose while machining without a fence in place. If there are no springs, remove the knobs, otherwise one could come out and strike the cutter.

Dust extraction

Fit extraction wherever possible and ensure that it is working. You can machine away quite merrily without realizing that the chippings are not being drawn up. This is worse than not fitting extraction at all, because the router will start to get jammed, with chippings flying around the cutter causing a hazard and a lot of dust.

Nowadays, most manufacturers pay reasonable attention to the need for extraction. This matters for safety, but also for keeping a tidy working environment and allowing the operator to see the progress of the cut. Most routers take add-on extraction pipes that are usually supplied with the machine. These are not ideal as the add-on parts tend to obscure the work, even though they are usually made of clear plastic, because dust sticks to them; inserting and removing the cutters can also prove to be awkward. The plastic is also likely to break or get lost eventually, so there has to be a better way. A number of routers, including the DeWalt 621, Triton machines and the Makita RP09, have proper built-in extraction, which is preferable.

An inverted router choked with softwood waste. Hardwood splinters do more damage.

Superior extraction

The best extractors I have found are the drum type that sit on the floor, perhaps tucked out of the way under a bench. Provided it has a large motor or motors, the drawing power is amazing; despite the large 100mm pipe diameter, it can lift a lot of chippings and dust from a router table as well as drawing off fine dust and chippings while jig working, using suitable branches to downsize the pipework if necessary. The open ends can be sited near the work or hooked up to the router's own extraction pipe, wherever gives the maximum effect.

However, you will find that many jigs clog up easily preventing the router from reaching the limit of its passes inside the jig. You may well need to switch off and lift the router off for a jig clean up between machining passes each time, which is a little tedious. You could then consider adding fixed extraction pipework between all your machines if the extractor is powerful enough. You can buy all the fittings, including blastgates and grounding kits to reduce static and therefore the risk of explosion that attends any build up of dust.

When standard extraction wouldn't do, I created my own base-fitted extraction device made from ultra-thin birch ply and plastic pipe for very dusty face-moulding work.

■ PORTABLE EXTRACTORS

For proper extraction, a small, mobile, portable extractor with automatic power-tool switching is a must. It allows fast and efficient working and deals with the majority of the waste. An ordinary vacuum cleaner is not suitable, though a small industrial model may fit the bill. The large router is at home in a table acting as a mini spindle-moulder – here the production of chippings can be vast, so a better answer than a small extractor is needed. A high-pressure, low-volume (HPLV) extractor may work well, despite the quantity of chippings, if a 'drop box' is fitted between the table and the extractor. The vacuum draws the chippings as far as the box where most dust settles while the lighter dust continues to the extractor. This is a cheap way to enlarge collection capacity.

A typical auto extractor. It has two switches: one is on/off; the other allows manual or auto switching triggered when the power tool plugged into it is itself switched on. There is a delay in the extractor switching itself off again so the dust can clear from the pipe into the extractor.

COMMON FAULTS WITH ROUTERS

No matter how carefully you work with the router, all machines will become worn or even damaged over time. Nowadays there are many more budget routers on the market. They are not necessarily as well made as one several times the price with a well-respected brand name. Such lower-price models can be a good way to get started in routing, but don't be surprised if such a machine fails early on. It may be better to regard such power tools as having a limited working life, to be replaced, hopefully, with a better-made unit. Budget routers tend to have small collets to hold the cutters, and cheaper bearings. They should not be used on really heavy work or very long or big cutters as they probably will not cope or, at least, a large cutter will vibrate badly.

Improper use of cutters is a common fault with new routers. Other possible faults might include switches, electronics or bearings that may have escaped factory inspection, but could show up after some use. These are typical long-term wear items anyway, so should a problem develop, it will usually be with one of those items.

Proper use of cutters

Routers are intended for quite heavy and punishing work, but they fare a lot better if used for the level of work for which they were built. If you attempt heavy, single-pass cuts with a lightweight model of around 600 watts or less, the strain will show after a while, even if it manages to see out the warranty period. The cutters won't like the abuse either, and neither will you. In fact you, the operator, are the best judge of how the machine is faring. If it is always under apparent strain and cannot cut quickly and efficiently and without some nasty accompanying noises, there is evidently something wrong. The question is, what? Cheap starter sets of cutters are not made for heavy work, neither are they worth having resharpened since there is too little carbide (the cutting-edge material) to make this practical.

Switch faults

The on/off switch of routers used to be very vulnerable to getting packed with dust and resin, especially from MDF (medium-density fibreboard). The switchblade contacts have a tendency to wear and will gradually burn away or stick together with repeated usage. However, many switches are now booted with a soft rubber cover to seal them against dust, so this is not so much of an issue as it used to be.

Faults in the electronics

The electronics control package for correct speed control can give out very suddenly, and after several hurried changes of fuse it becomes obvious that a visit to the repair shop is unavoidable. Motor brushes do eventually wear out; this wear can normally be observed by removing the case or brush covers. If changing them is easy, according to the manual, then there is no reason why you shouldn't attempt this. However, some machines have an intricate arrangement for locating the brushes, so it is safer to pass this job on to an expert. For some reason, many cheap routers come with spare motor brushes even though these machines are unlikely to last long enough to warrant a change of brushes.

Replacing motor brushes is sometimes made easy if there are screw-in covers on the motor housing. However, you will rarely have to do this.

■ FAULTY ROUTERS

If you suspect that a new router is going wrong, contact the dealer who sold it to you. At the very least, he may be able to tell you whether you are doing something incorrectly, but equally he must get the machine repaired or replaced if it is at fault. I was once sold a very large, well-known brand of router only to discover that it ran at only half-speed and produced a long and pretty trail of bright blue arcing running around the commutator, where the fault lay.

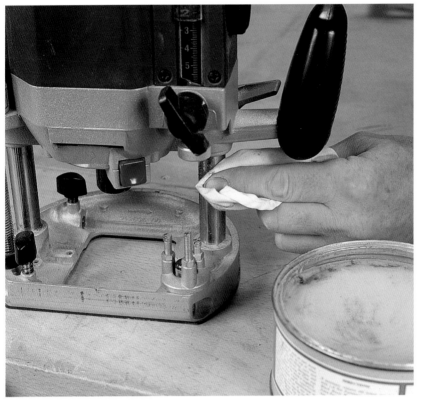

Waxing the plunge columns makes plunging smooth and easy.

★ **WORKING TIP**

Owning a router or two can result in various odd bits and pieces from collets to nuts and bolts and anti-vibration springs, not to mention spanners. I use a large-size plastic toolbox with a lift-out tray big enough to store all my routing miscellanea so I am never stuck when I need to find a part or do a minor repair. The kit can include things like collet cleaning brushes and dry lubricant too. You can store extraction fittings and even the router fence if it is large enough, ready to go anywhere.

Replacing bearings

Routers have two bearings on the motor shaft. There is normally a large, heavy-duty one at the business end and a smaller one at the top. These bearings are normally sealed and are a special high-speed type, so if they need replacing, it is essential that the same type is fitted. This should be done by an experienced person; removing and returning the motor shaft, and all the other parts that get in the way, in the right order and undamaged, is a tricky job.

Lubricating plunge columns

On plunge-type routers it is necessary to lubricate the plunge columns. I find that a machine wax (as opposed to a water-based one) is good on columns as oil tends to attract dust. Lubricated columns allow easy plunging and avoid aggressive contact with the workpiece when forcing it down too hard. WD 40 or silicone spray lubricant also works. Don't let it get on your workpiece, however, as it can repel any finish you might apply later.

Working safely with the router table is covered within Chapter 7, but you should follow the manufacturer's recommendations as to whether a cutter should be used freehand or in a table. Cutter catalogues normally show which large cutters are for static use only or whether a machine with minimum motor wattage is required, along with the maximum safe operating speed.

OPERATIONAL SAFETY

Safety should come as standard with any work process; however, there are plenty of woodworkers sporting injuries, so clearly things do not always go well. Think through each operation before you start and try to get an understanding from your own experience as to how cutting force, feed direction, speed under load and depth of cut all affect your work. Make sure you keep your fingers away from cutters and use sensible means of work guidance such as fences and push blocks rather than relying on luck.

Direction of cut

It is vital to feed the cutter into the work in the correct direction when working on the edge of a workpiece. The feed direction must be against the rotation of the cutter. When machining in the middle of a board, you don't have to concern yourself with this. However, when you widen such a cut, the second pass must obey the direction-of-cut rule.

Table or freehand working

Some work is only possible freehand; other tasks can be carried out either freehand or on a router table, and still other jobs can only be done on a table. There are several reasons for this. First, there is the size (or lack of it) and stability of the workpiece. If the workpiece is fixed, you have no choice but to machine in situ. Safety is an obvious issue, but so is the quality of the result. Generally speaking, a decent-size table will allow the wood to pass smoothly over the cutter, giving good control and therefore a good finish. It is also safer to machine small sections in this way. There are various techniques for dealing with small or awkward sections; these are covered in Chapter 7 (see p. 110).

Freehand working can mean unintended 'stepping' or damage at the start or finish of a cut where the moulding runs right through and the router is not stable enough. This happens, for instance, when doing edge work. Extending the running surface can help with this. If you need to protect the inverted face of a workpiece, use something with non-slip protection such as the Routermat or similar product; these can be bought at do-it-yourself and hardware stores. There are also special rubber-faced work supports available, such as Loc Blocks or Bench Cookies.

It pays to not only appreciate how to work safely, but also to use the router appropriately. That is to say, work freehand when that is correct and use the correct form of guidance, perhaps a guide bush, not necessarily the ubiquitous straight fence, or use a router table when that is the better method, with its improved control and ability to machine small or awkward components. Basically, the table-mounted router is already tamed and fairly well under control as it is fixed and the workpiece offered up to it, but the freehand machine is often just that, too free in use to be properly controllable.

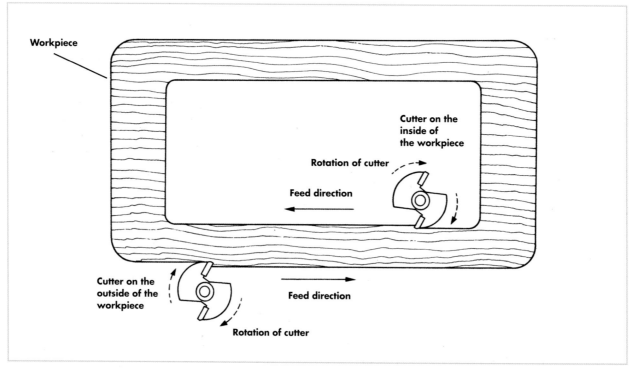

The direction of cut. A plan view of internal and external passes.

A straight piece of batten is clamped in place to allow accurate edge-planing of a ply board.

Non-slip mats make freehand routing safe, even without the use of clamps.

★ WORKING TIP

A recent discovery of mine is using waste pieces of polyurethane insulation board. This material is normally foil-wrapped and fitted into new-build cavity walls and roof spaces between rafters. It is perfect for machining on as the cutter finds no resistance when it breaks through and there is no flying dust. Use spray adhesive to temporarily hold the workpiece down.

■ ROUTER TABLE SAFETY

This subject is covered fully in Chapter 7, but suffice to say that proper guarding and the use of hold-downs to control the work are essential. Proprietary tables should come with these, while homemade ones can have all these parts made to suit the table.

CUTTER SAFETY

There are a number of safety aspects to be aware of when working with cutters. For example, it is easy to forget to switch off the router before changing the cutter – we've all done it at some time or other, but it's nothing to be proud of. With 18,000–24,000rpm and up to 2,000 watts of power, a router is a dangerous animal. Get into the habit of switching it off and unplugging it. If you unplug, your safety is guaranteed; switching off alone is not enough.

Collet care

The collet, which is held onto the motor spindle of the router by the collet nut, is intimately connected to the shank of any cutter that you might use. Because of this, the safe use of any cutter is dependant on the state of the collet.

If you do a lot of routing it is advisable to change your collets at least once a year. Worn collets are dangerous because cutters can come loose and fly out. If you find that the cutter is slipping, this will usually be the cause. The dynamic forces of machining can cause the collet to 'spread' or become oval, which means that it will not grip a cutter shank properly. Good collets are expensive because of the fine machining required and the quality of the steel. However, not replacing a faulty one could cost you more.

If the collet does not stay locked into the collet nut when the whole assembly is undone, the O ring (if fitted) may need to be replaced (N.B. some routers are intended to have loose collets). Cheap routers have quite small lesser-quality collets – these should not be overstressed by using large or long cutters.

More frequent replacement may be necessary if the collet wears more quickly. A key point is that the collet must always match the shank size, since a collet does not have movable jaws like a drill chuck and the cutter speed is of course very high, with consequently higher risk.

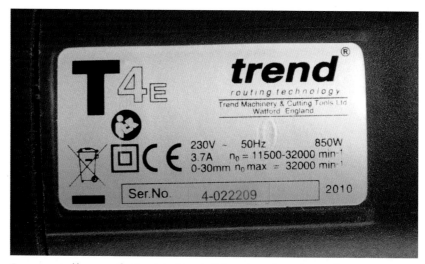

Every power tool has a specification plate giving vital information such as voltage and input wattage and serial number.

Globally, there are a variety of collet sizes, making it possible to confuse metric and imperial sizes. An example would be trying to fit a European 12mm shanked cutter in a standard UK/US ½in collet. The 0.7mm difference with the collet nut tightened up would be enough to wreck the collet and still cause the cutter to fly out at high speed. Generally it is wise to check that all your collets and cutter shanks are truly compatible – vernier callipers are handy for checking shanks and collets.

Cutter selection and use

Always buy new cutters from well-known high-quality brands. If you are offered any used cutters, be cautious. They may look alright, but you could be buying something of dubious quality that has done a lot of mileage or may have been dropped, which can break or loosen the inserts on TCT (tungsten-carbide-tipped) bits, or the shanks may be damaged or bent from misuse. Tungsten-carbide tips often look and feel sharp but have in fact lost their edge. In other words, never buy a secondhand cutter, even from a friend – it is far too risky.

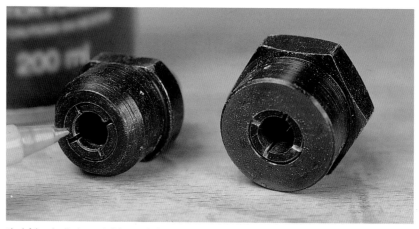

The left-hand collet has a slightly rounded-out mouth where a cutter has slid right out during machining. This means it will no longer grip properly. The right-hand collet is still in good condition.

Cutter care

Cutters, just like collets, require care; you need to check regularly that they are still fit for use. In particular, they should be sharp. This is a matter of judgement based on visual observation and performance. Does the cutting edge look blunt? Does it look as if it has accumulated burnt deposits or a build-up of resin? Are there nicks in the edges of the blade or are pieces missing? Is it hard work making a pass with the cutter and does the wood burn when you do so?

If any of your answers to the above questions are positive, then it may be time for a regrind, or even time to throw the cutter away if the damage is severe or if it has reached its limit. Cheap cutters have thin cutting edges and are not fit for regrinding.

Cutter types

The choice is basically between HSS (high-speed steel) or TCT (tungsten-carbide-tipped) cutters. The former are good to use on softwoods, being intrinsically sharper to start with, but go blunt fairly quickly. They have virtually been replaced by TCT cutters, which are much better for general work, especially in hardwoods and MDF. HSS cutters have a more integral construction, being formed from a solid piece of steel, whereas the TCT cutter has brittle, sintered (powdered, granular metal compressed under high temperature) cutting edges that are brazed on. This is fine most of the time, but damage to the edges, a weak piece of brazing, or a fall to the workshop floor can leave the cutter in a dangerous state.

The cutter on the left is in good order, while the one on the right shows a worn insert, broken corners, nicked edges and a build-up of resin and dirt.

Cleaning a cutter

Take any suspect cutter and thoroughly clean the debris from it with white spirit or lighter fuel and a piece of scourer or the edge of a trimming knife blade. This should be done regularly in any case, because cutting efficiency is reduced by a build-up of grime. Take care not to cut yourself when doing this.

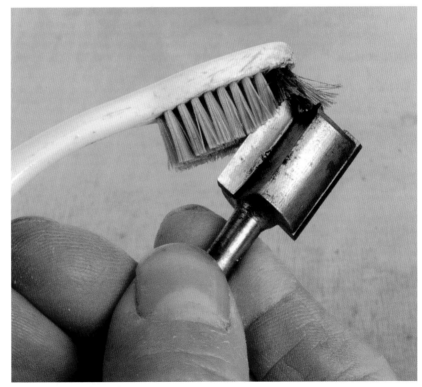

Take care not to nick yourself on sharp cutter edges when cleaning. Use a wax cleaning agent or blade cleaner. An old toothbrush is good for this task, but keep the work away from your face in case you get splashes in your eyes.

Honing a cutter

It is possible to hone the flat face of a TCT cutter with a diamond hone, although you should not attempt this unless you are confident you can restore the cutting edge properly without affecting the efficiency of the cutter. Honing is the very fine sharpening of a cutter, not to be confused with grinding, which is a more serious removal of the cutting edge to get back to a good, clean, sharp edge. You can send a blunt cutter to a saw doctor, but the cost of many discount cutters means that it is sometimes just as cheap to discard the cutter and buy a new one.

Shank problems

Other cutter problems can be the result of marked and damaged, or even bent, shanks. An expert at Trend Machinery (UK) told me that a 'rising cutter', where the cutter starts to slide out of the collet under load, is caused exclusively by worn collets. Replace the collet in question if this seems to be the case (professional users need to change heavily used collets once a year; amateur users will not need to do this quite so often). Taking this step will protect your other cutters as well as yourself.

If you can see that a shank is badly marked or worn, then it really is damaged and should be thrown away. Bent shanks are also a liability; ¼in shank cutters can bend if they are asked to do too much; throw them away immediately.

Storing cutters

Cutters should always be kept apart and in a special box or compartment designated for them. If the edges touch, they can be damaged because they are so brittle. It is worth having a proper pouch or box for each one.

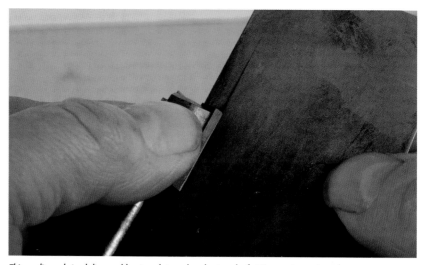

This credit-card-sized diamond-honing plate makes short work of giving a crisp cutting edge. Use water as the lubricant.

Reground cutters

Any cutter that is reground is left with the mass of the backing steel uncomfortably close to the edge of the carbide and a point is reached where grinding the steel back is the only solution for longer life. This should be done only to cutters that are large and expensive enough to warrant it, but it is strictly a job for a saw doctor, as dynamic balancing is critical for safety. The result of all regrinding is a reduction in the size of the cutter profile and possible loss of shape. Matched profile-and-scribe cutter sets and the like may not function properly after such attention. If in doubt, discuss it with the saw doctor first.

Multiple passes

Taking multiple passes will avoid bent shanks, cutter slippage, and a strained motor and bearings and will, of course, produce a good piece of work without tearout, burns and severe chatter-marking.

This cutter had a completely straight shank before it slipped out of the collet. The cutter itself may still be usable, but the bent shank is too badly damaged. Note, too, the wasted end of the shank.

■ MACHINE SIZE

Less experienced woodworkers will often ask: What cutter should I use? What size shank is best to go for? Which machine should I use? Popular advice to such users is: 'get a big router'. That's fine, but a ½in collet router costs a lot of money, and if you don't intend to use it a great deal there isn't much point in owning one. A small router is much easier to handle, the controls are easier to operate and the standard of the work can be finer. Such a machine can also be successfully inverted in a table.

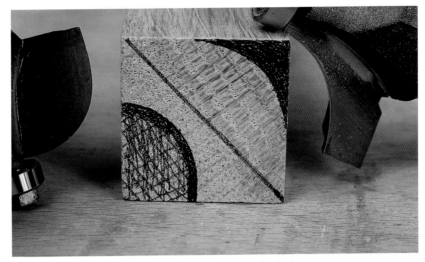

A comparison of cove and roundover cutters shows the large bite taken by the cove cutter.

Setting the depth

Some cutters, such as the roundover, don't take out too much even at full depth. However, the opposite profile, the cove bit, which comes with a bearing (unlike the similarly shaped core box, which doesn't), takes out a substantial bite and needs to be applied in stages to avoid trouble. Erring on the side of safety means that a ¼in shanked cutter should only take out a depth of cut equal to the width of the shank. This isn't entirely realistic, as the example of roundover versus cove shows, and common sense needs to be applied when depth setting. The three-stage turret fitted to a router is invaluable for this work and can usually be adjusted to optimize the depth of passes you can take. There are several routers fitted with multi-stage turrets allowing accurate multiple passes, which can be handy in this sort of situation.

Depth setting with the ½in collet router

The ½in collet router is much better suited to heavy and intensive work. Compared to ¼in shank cutters, the ½in shank cutters have shanks that are disproportionately larger than a mere doubling of the diameter. This gives a tremendous boost to cutter size and design as well as the amount that can be cut away in one go. There are some pretty scary-looking cutters for panel raising, cornice and handrail production, but these can only be used in a router table at low speed (10,000rpm maximum), using an electronic router. Correct speed is vital, not just for the safety of the operator but also to keep TCT cutters intact. The ½in shanked cutters rarely bend. However, the cutter can start to slide out with heavy passes if the collet has worn.

¼in, 8mm and ½in shanked cutters. The ½in has a much larger cutting profile.

CHAPTER 4

ROUTER CUTTERS

The router is nothing without cutters. I find that choosing and using the cutters is the most interesting and rewarding part of the job. Since I first started in woodworking there has been a huge increase in the variety and type of cutters available. In this chapter, I start by examining the construction of a typical cutter and then examine the basic differences between HSS, TCT, diamond cutters and disposable-tip types. Then I run through the entire 'cast list' of cutters that are available on the market today. The variety is staggering.

It is a legal requirement in the European Union that tooling of all kinds has safety markings; this includes router cutters. The latest versions of the cutters shown in this chapter should bear these markings laser-etched onto the shanks, including a collet depth mark that indicates the amount of shank that should be inserted in the collet. The collet depth mark is a definite safety improvement.

CUTTER MANUFACTURE

Most router cutters on the market are of good quality. Beware of the very cheap deals: the cutters may be of inferior quality with thin carbide, poor brazing, and cutters that cannot be plunged because they lack a bottom cutting insert. None of these things should be an issue with a well-known brand. Start with a limited set of cutters rather than buying a really large set unless you are sure you will find all the cutters useful. It is better to add individual cutters as you need them.

High-speed steel (HSS) cutters

These are now fairly rare, having been largely ousted by the TCT cutter, which is a much better all-round performer. Note the sweeping waveform of the HSS cutter. This allows for easy clearance of chippings. Nevertheless, the HSS variety is quite nice to use. These cutters work best on softwoods, because hardwoods and manmade boards, such as MDF, will destroy the cutting edge quickly. Each cutter is machined from a one-piece steel blank and has two cutting edges. It may have a bottom cutting edge or edges machined into it. The initial sharpness of the edge is superior to that of a TCT, but this can get lost quite quickly. TCT has a much longer cutting life between sharpenings. Honing an HSS cutter is easy, although, as always, you need to keep to the original grinding angle if it is to cut properly. Regrinding is a job for a saw doctor.

Tungstern-carbide-tipped (TCT) cutters

Now by far the most readily available cutter type, the TCT seems to enjoy all the advantages, with just a few drawbacks. Tungsten carbide is a very tough metal that is sintered to form a blank. Sintering is a process whereby the grains of TCT are compressed and stuck together under high temperature. It follows that the resulting blank does not have the integrity of drawn or cast steel, and TCT is therefore rather brittle. Some cutters sourced from Asia are inferior-grade, having poor-quality TCT brazed inserts. These have a coarse-grain structure and the brazing itself may not be well done, leaving some serious weaknesses. The result can be that cutter inserts may fragment or break off completely. Also any cutter, however good, if dropped or brought into contact with another TCT cutter may fracture or chip quite easily, so careful, separate storage of cutters is important. Good-quality cutters use micrograin carbide cutter blanks, which are stronger and give a better edge. Generally, it is only the smaller sizes of cutter that are made entirely of TCT.

On the left is an HSS (high-speed steel) cutter intended for softwood with its characteristic waveform shape. On the right is a good-quality TCT (tungsten carbide-tipped) cutter with thick TCT blanks and clean brazing to the body.

This is due to the high cost of TCT compared to steel, which makes up the body of most TCT cutters. The steel also has the advantage of not being nearly so brittle and allows the shank to bend and give a little under stress, which is safer. There are two

grades of cutter: the light do-it-yourself type, and the heavy-duty professional sort. The difference is in the build quality. Amateur versions have thinner carbide tips and less steel in the body of the cutter. It all depends on what you expect to use your cutters for. For occasional use, the light cutters are fine, although they come in a limited number of moulding styles. The heavy-duty cutters will allow several resharpenings before they have to be ditched, but that will be after an immense amount of work in many cases.

TCT is intrinsically slightly blunter than HSS because of its granular nature. However, its ability to keep cutting successfully can be amazing, though it becomes a little hard to judge whether the edge has lost its keenness or not.

It pays to store your cutters neatly for identification and safely so they do not chip their cutting edges.

Polycrystalline diamond (PCD) cutters

Studies of TCT cutters working at high speeds have shown that because of the high temperatures involved when cutting is in progress, TCT actually 'melts' and the edge rounds over a tiny amount. Clearly, however successful TCT has been, there is still a need to find some superior material for very demanding applications. One experiment was to use ceramic cutters; these are capable of resisting high temperatures, but have some inherent drawbacks, not the least of which is their brittleness, which is greater than that of TCT. For some time now, diamond-faced cutters have been available for difficult professional applications. These are not intended for amateur use, because they are expensive and unsuitable; they can only be used in large fixed-head machines. The diamonds used are nothing like jewellery diamonds and are microfine, being coated all over with cutting faces.

Replaceable-tip cutters

These TCT cutters are used a lot by professionals who tend to demolish sharp edges through the sheer amount of work they do, especially with MDF. Basically, the cutter has a shank and a body as usual, but the body is machined to take disposable blades. These are safely located and held down with Torx or Allen screws.

One key advantage is that the cutting diameter always stays the same since no resharpening is involved. However, they are limited to simple profiles, because these are the ones most often used for repetitive cutting. Replaceablet-tip cutters are of academic interest to the beginner, especially as there are plenty of good-quality discount TCT cutters on the market, which last a long time in less demanding hands.

A PCD cutter.

A replaceable-tip cutter is cheaper in the long run, as you can turn the cutting edges round or replace as necessary.

STRAIGHT CUTTERS

These are the first and most basic types of cutter that anyone uses. There is quite a lot to them, however, as they come in several varieties and in an enormous range of sizes. Depending on the type, sizes range from a single-flute cutter of just 1/16in (1.5mm) diameter up to a two-flute cutter with a huge 11 5/16in (50mm) diameter. Actual cutter lengths go from a mere 1/4in up to about 11 5/16in (5–50mm), although cutters for deep mortising can be even longer. Considering the rather straightforward nature of these cutters' tasks, there is a surprising variety. (See page 71 for some more unusual types.) Although I don't give an exhaustive list of applications, the straight cutter is anything but limited – it is the most useful of all the cutters you are likely to own.

The two-flute straight cutter

We start with the standard two-flute pattern, which, as its name suggests, has two cutting edges. This is the best type to use, because it gives a good finish and is quite strong. It may also have a bottom cutter or insert so that it can be plunged into the work successfully.

An open tongue-and-groove joint.

A small straight cutter is used to make slots for inlaying bandings.

A long straight cutter in a big router, machining a mortise for a strong, reliable joint.

Grooving a cabinet to take a thin back panel.

Rebating using the fence to guide the cutter.

■ THE MANY USES OF STRAIGHT CUTTERS

Straight cutters are capable of many tasks; they are less limited in scope than moulding cutters, which have just one profile and very particular applications. The following list shows the range of jobs they can undertake:

- Applying inlay and stringing to boxes or furniture

- Machining frets on electric guitars

- Carving fine detail and shapes freehand

- Trimming boards to size

- Planing edges

- Producing slots of any width

- Producing rebates (steps)

- Adding decorative detail

- Making slots on board edges

- Making loose tongue-and-groove joints

- Making finger joints on boxes

- Making a groove for a weather seal on a window frame

- Producing classical dentil (tooth-pattern) moulding

- Fitting back panels into kitchen cabinets

- Drilling holes

- Making mortises for table and chair legs

- Making mortises for door locks

- Working with templates

- Making grooves that can then be followed by a bearing-guided moulding cutter

A variety of two-flute straight cutters. The far-right green one has a depth scale on the cutter, while third from the right the cutter has thick chip-limiting shoulders.

The single-flute straight cutter

The next sort is the single-flute cutter, which does not give as good a finish as the two-flute version since it can take only half the number of cuts at any given speed. However, it does clear away the chippings more efficiently and is available in very small sizes. For a beginner it is perhaps less suitable than the two-flute cutter, unless you have a specific need for a single-flute one.

The down shear cutter

We now come to the more exotic cutters, such as the down shear and up-down shear, which has angled blades to slice through veneered or solid wood without 'spelching' or breakout. This is a term I use often; it refers to the tearing of the wood when a cutter moves across the grain. Woodworkers are always seeking to avoid this, because it looks so bad on a finished piece of work (for more details, see Chapter 7).

The hinge recesser

This is a rather likeable little cutter, popular with many cabinetmakers. It is a small, straight cutter with the centre missing at the end of it. This allows good clearance for chippings when making shallow recesses such as those required for hinges.

The stagger-tooth cutter

Lastly, we have the stagger-tooth and pocket cutters. These are normally quite long and can sometimes be used at a greater depth than the length of the cutting edge might suggest. The reason for this is that some of the shank can enter the pocket or mortise, providing that plenty of passes are taken in order to reduce the strain on the cutter. They are available in small sizes for ¼in routers, and much larger ones for ½in machines. You need to be doing some serious work to want one of these cutters, because they can give you a bumpy ride!

Back row: from left to right, stagger-tooth, pocket, down shear, up-down shear.
Front row: from left to right, down shear, hinge mortise.

ROUNDOVER/OVOLO CUTTERS

The next cutters on the list are the roundovers/ovolos. These are less functional, but offer a very basic start for decorative moulding. They can be used to follow on from a straight cutter. You might start with a nice square edge or groove and then elect to use the roundover to produce a profile off that. The term 'roundover' is self-explanatory; 'ovolo' is a traditional term for a regular convex curve with one or two small shoulders or steps. This adds a certain classical decoration that the pure roundover on its own does not.

The same cutter can produce either a roundover or an ovolo – the only difference being the size of the bearing used to guide it along the workpiece. A bearing smaller than the cutter edge ensures that the step is cut. Equally, setting the cutter down below the flush height of the work will ensure that the other step is also cut. The roundover is good for modern work, whereas the ovolo looks more comfortable with reproduction styling.

One advantage of an ovolo cut is that it can be used to mask slight surface discrepancies, such as those between a veneered board and a 'planted on' solid lipping that needs moulded decoration. Don't buy cutters that come with just a guide pin or pilot, because they will burn, or even dent the wood, due to friction. The only good reason for using pin-guided cutters is to follow intricate shapes that a bearing cannot do well because of its larger diameter. This applies to most types of cutter; instead choose a cutter that will take interchangeable bearings, perhaps in several sizes. This will allow one cutter to do several different jobs. Cutter sizes can vary between a mere ⅛in (3.2mm) radius up to about 1½in (38mm) for use in static set-ups. The smaller sizes are fine for the beginner.

Roundover/ovolo cutters. Different bearings determine the resultant step, or no step, as the case may be.

A roundover cutter being used to radius an edge. Note the support for the router base to prevent tipping.

COVE AND COREBOX CUTTERS

These two are the opposite of the roundover/ovolo, because they produce concave rather than convex mouldings. Unlike roundover/ovolo cutters, however, these two cutter patterns are quite separate types, for technical reasons. Both have disadvantages compared to the roundover/ovolo. The main one is the amount that they have to remove when cutting. If you take a small, square section of wood and draw a diagonal from one corner to the other, then hold a roundover on the end face, it is apparent that only a small amount of wood will be removed to form the moulding. However, if you hold a cove cutter in place, you can see that most of the square section will be cut away to make the profile.

The dynamics involved mean that a lot more stress is applied to both router cutter and workpiece. The finish will also be bad. To avoid straining the motor and possibly bending the cutter shank, the sensible course is to make several passes. The steps will not be constant ones, as the first pass will take out relatively little, while the successive passes will remove much more. A little common sense is needed when setting the depth each time.

Unlike the cove, the corebox cutter has no bearing. This means that it can be used for bottom-cutting work. The downside here is that if you look at the very centre of the cutter tip, it will be apparent that the two opposing

cutting edges meet. Simple science tells us that the smaller the diameter of an object, the lower the speed. Therefore, at a cutter's outer edge it will be travelling fast, but at the centre it is going relatively slowly. In fact, at the very centre (probably an atom's width), the cutter is actually standing still. In practical terms, this means that a cutter travelling slowly causes more friction, is more likely to burn the workpiece, and will not be able to move in a straight line properly. Corebox cutters are very useful, but they do need to be sharp and, as always with fence work, you need to pull the router towards you so it is less likely to wander off. Lastly, don't linger in one place with a corebox cutter, because it will burn the workpiece.

Cove and corebox cutters. The smaller sizes are the most useful ones.

REBATE CUTTERS

The rebate cutter, or in old parlance 'rabbet' (from the French 'rabot' or 'plane'), is invaluable as a basic cutter and should be included in any set. Unlike the straight cutter, the rebate has a shallow cutting depth but a wider diameter due to the guide pin or bearing. I should explain that cutters don't automatically come with or without bearings; in some cases they can take a bearing as an optional item. In this case, a rebater isn't truly a rebater without some sort of guidance. What makes it so useful is its ability to accurately take the corner out of a square profile and follow the contour of the workpiece whatever shape it is. Thus a task such as rebating the back of an assembled mirror frame is easy: if you have different-sized rebaters, it is possible to cut a second step for the board that will cover the mirror and hold it in place (see right).

Of course, rebaters have many other uses. As with all guided cutters, the rebater will follow any defects in the wood, so a missing knot or tearout will result in a kink in the line of the rebate. Any such faults should be made good before machining. Nowadays it is possible to get a

Stepped rebates. The one on the left would be suitable for holding glass and backing in a picture frame, while the other is intended to hold 'Tonk' or library strip for supporting shelves.

large rebater and a set of bearings to cover all useful sizes of rebate. It is a very handy cutter to have.

A selection of rebaters including a CMT 'Master Rebate Set' (multi-bearing type).

TRIMMERS

These are for making one surface flush with another. An example would be levelling a solid strip inset into a tabletop, or perhaps neatly finishing the laminate on a kitchen worktop. Trimmers vary in length.

The large ones are ideal for heavy, templated profile work such as electric-guitar bodies or dining-chair legs. Most are straight, although some are bevelled or double bevelled for laminate trimming in either one or two passes. Unless you are intending to do a lot of worktop trimming, the long profile pattern is probably more useful.

Heavy-profile work. Note the burns on the upper part due to cutter wear from template working. 'Sticky' gloves give a non-slip grip.

Back row: from left to right, three template trimmers, five panel trimmers.
Front row: from left to right, pierce and trim, laminiate trim, surface trim, two laminate trimmers, rota-tip.

BEADS AND REEDS

These are other examples of traditional or classical moulding shapes that have transferred successfully to modern routing technology. The bead is a single roundover shape that can be semicircular in profile and is usually accompanied by at least one shoulder. There are various types, such as the staff bead, the corner bead and the sunk bead. The bead can be extended in profile by the addition of other features, as with the staff bead (see right). The corner-bead variety usually has a bearing, although the other types may not. The reverse (concave) type of cutter is also available.

Where several small beads are grouped together to form a more intricate profile, it becomes a 'reed' cutter. This more delicate effect has many uses, such as on chair legs and table edges and for generally prettying up otherwise plain surfaces.

Bead cutters have their own uses, being very suitable for the edges of window ledges and cabinets. The corner bead is ideal for corner detail on legs and also to form a door bead where two doors meet. In this situation, two flat surfaces together often look plain; if they are not level, or if the gap between them is unequal, it shows. The bead cutter is another useful item to have in a basic set.

From left to right: edge bead, staff bead, sunk bead, reeding and fluting (the reverse effect).

Back row: from left to right, edge beads, sunk mould, cove and bead, three beads.
Front row: from left to right, two reeds, fluting.

EDGE AND DECORATIVE MOULDS

These form a group of cutters that add useful detail to an exposed plain edge or surface. Included in the group are some of the bead, reed and ovolo cutters already mentioned, as well as some more exotic varieties. These cutters are often elaborate and large, but they add substantial amounts of moulding detail that would otherwise be lacking. Unfortunately, some need a ½in collet router. Also, most of them are traditional profiles that do not look appropriate with modern styling. One cutter of note is the bolection. Among other things, it is often added for detail around panels in frame and panel construction. This is one group of cutters that has benefited from the revival of traditional moulding plane profiles such as the lamb's tongue.

Various edge moulds, including cavetto (top left), thumb mould (bottom left) and bolection (top right), complete with a rebate on the underside to allow it to sit on a square frame edge.

Back row: from left to right, thumb mould, guided bead ovolo, bolection, bullnose.
Front row: from left to right, cavetto, guided classic ogee, guided off-set classic mould, classic profile, classical bead, classic decorative bead.

JOINTERS

Some jointing cutters can be purely functional, while others, such as the profile-and-scribe cutter, also lend aesthetic details to the workpiece. The glue-joint cutter provides a positive and extremely solid joint between edges. There are one or two drawbacks, however. First, like most joint cutters, it is only available with a ½in shank. Second, it is necessary to prepare the components carefully. The two opposing faces of the joint are both machined face down on the router table – one must then be reversed to assemble the joint. This means that the thickness of everything has to be exact if you are to end up with a level or flush joint. The edges need to be planed true as well. Wood being wood, it can still change shape overnight; when this happens, persuading it to run absolutely flat across the router table is quite difficult.

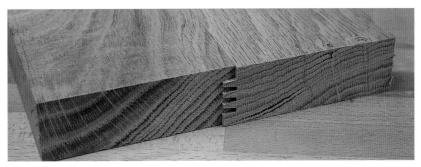

An assembled finger joint.

Often, the wood will require sanding with a belt sander to level any inconsistencies after assembly.

Joints need to be defluffed with abrasive paper, lightly glued and strongly clamped to be successful. The result is impossible to break, however, and is ideal for things such as multi-strip kitchen worktops, butchers' blocks and the like.

There are other jointers, such as the lock-mitre, which is used in drawer-box construction. Again, the work benefits from careful preparation, machining and assembly. Lastly, there are one or two classical panel sets available. They are not the full 'profile-and-scribe' type, which have decoration, but they form part of a joint construction after the tenon-and-groove part of the joint has been cut separately.

Back row: from left to right, two finger joints, lock mitre.
Front row: from left to right, two glue joints.

CHAMFER AND V-GROOVE

Both of these cutters provide a simple way to add detail to nearly anything. The chamfer is bearing-guided and tends to give a cut of 45° or steeper. It is perfect for following a shape and is effective for creating stopped chamfers on all kinds of woodwork including in-situ work – on a square newel post, for example. The V-groove, on the other hand, has a point and no means of guidance apart from the router fence, and is good for adding surface detailing. It can be used freehand or with a template for carving or making a name plaque for a house. Each has a place in a basic cutter set.

A V-point or bevel cutter. It has been used to bevel the reverse of some oak panels for a linen chest.

Clockwise from back left: three bevel cutters that will accept bearings, bearing-guided chamfer cutter, laser-point cutter for freehand carving, another bearing-guided chamfer cutter and two V-groove cutters.

DOVETAIL

The role of the dovetail router cutter has expanded over the years. It now comes in sizes and varieties to suit anything from cutting stair trenchings and housings (to create complete staircases) to the construction of small boxes. Some cutters are designed to work with specific dovetail jigs, such as the Leigh or Incra jigs. The results produced can be awe-inspiring pieces of fine cabinetwork, but of course these jigs have a price tag to match. There are simpler jigs available (see Chapter 9), which can be useful if you are keen to make dovetailed joints. Dovetail cutters can also make housing joints, which are a very strong method of carcass construction.

The very best machine-cut dovetails can look as good as this handcut example.

A selection of dovetail cutters. The one on the left is for stair housings. The small to medium sizes are the most useful. Many dovetail jigs need cutters to exactly match the jig.

PROFILE AND SCRIBE

The advent of this type of matched cutter set meant that for lightweight cabinet doors, conventional mortise-and-tenon joints, or the less-effective dowel joint, were no longer necessary. What is more, there are a number of different moulding profiles available. The moulding holds the centre panel in a slot behind, which also forms one half of the joint. A scribing cutter is used to form the other part of the joint and the counter profile, which plugs into the other component. This is needed four times to make a complete door frame, but in practice it is fairly quick – all the scribing cuts are done first and then all of the profile cuts. The frame is completed by a light sanding and gluing up. You need a panel-raising cutter to make the panel. The panel is inserted before the frame is glued up. The results are efficiently made, strong and attractive doors. The various moulding styles include bevel, ogee and classical. These sets are only available in 8mm and ½in shanked versions.

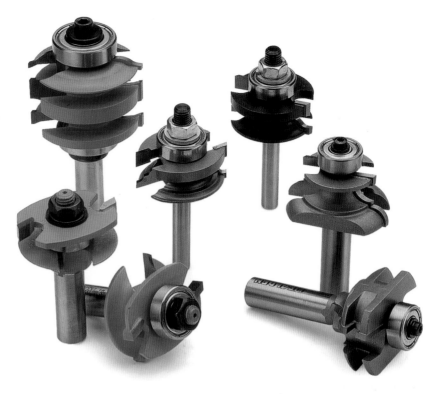

Back row: from left to right, CMT combination cutter, two Wealden reversible sets. Front row: from left to right, CMT two-piece set, large two-piece set.

PANEL CUTTERS

These come in two types: the panel raiser, which produces a panel to fit in a door frame, for example, and the face mould, which applies a moulded effect into the face of a board. This could be used in a variety of ways: to break up a plain surface or to decorate the edge of a drawer front. The largest sizes of panel cutter will only fit into a ½in router, but the smaller types will fit an 8mm collet on a smaller machine. The panel raiser is available as both a large flat-type cutter or a smaller vertical-type that will fit into small router table openings. In fact, most should be mounted in a router table for safety. The small face-mould patterns work well for decoration and one could be included in a basic set of cutters.

Face moulds, designed to cut into the face of a workpiece. Some work with templates using a bearing.

Panel raisers, which are among the largest cutters available. The vertical types can be used in smaller routers, although the orange CMT cutter also shapes the reverse side.

SLOTTERS

Slot cutters or groovers are for functional rather than decorative use. In effect, they are like mini saw blades with just two, three or four teeth. However, they are more versatile than this suggests. For a start, they normally fit onto an arbor, or shaft. This shaft can usually take a combination of these cutters with exact and adjustable spacing in between if required. They vary in thickness from 1/16 to 7/16in (1.5–11mm), while the diameters run from 1⅜ to 11⁵/₁₆in (36–50mm), or even to 31⁵/₁₆in (100mm) exceptionally. Another feature of these is that you can put bearings on the arbor.

These cutters can be used to make tongue-and-groove jointing and matchboarding (sometimes called TGV – tongue, groove and V) when teamed up with a bevel cutter on the same arbor. They are also useful for biscuit jointing and for slotting window frames to take weather seals. In the last role, the cutter and the arbor have to be special threaded types, thus allowing you to cut flush to the inside of the frame without the usual projecting shaft and nut. The biscuit-jointing option is interesting because, for a reasonable cost, it is possible to perform many of the jointing operations that would normally need a separate biscuit-jointing machine. It isn't quite as quick or convenient, but it is a good substitute and has an advantage over a jointer in that it can be used on curves or angled shapes.

Slotters and biscuit cutters. Arbors, groovers, bearings and spacers are all interchangeable and cutters can be ganged on ½in arbors.

MINIATURE CUTTERS

These cutters are used to make miniature-sized mouldings for dolls' houses. This is a popular activity and these cutters make it possible not only to make the dolls' house itself with full-size cutters, but also to do all the joinery and second fixings as well at 1/12 scale to match the scale of the dolls' house. A lightweight router of 400–600 watts is sufficient, as these cutters remove only a tiny amount of wood. All the typical mouldings are there, including skirting, dado, cornice and beading. The technique with these cutters is the same as with any small moulding. You machine the edge of a wide board and saw the moulding off using a fine blade on the circular saw, repeating as many times as is necessary to get the required quantity of moulding.

A selection of miniature cutters. The full-size torus cutter at the back gives an indication of scale.

CORNICE CUTTERS

Most pieces of full-height cabinet furniture, including kitchen cupboards and wardrobes, are topped off with a finishing moulding known as a cornice. This projects outwards and lends the work a look of importance and completeness as well as being an attractive detail. There are now plenty of cutters for this purpose and they tend to be fairly large. They can be 2½in (60mm) long, depending on the pattern, so they are strictly for the large router. In lieu of such a machine, or cutter for that matter, it is possible to build up a cornice in stages, moulding each stage on a separate piece of board before gluing the various pieces together.

A built-up cornice, using just two moulding profiles.

Cornice cutters. These are strictly for large routers, but the results are impressive.

OGEE CUTTERS

The ogee is a classical shape that has survived into the 21st century. The two basic patterns are the Roman and the Grecian. The Roman is a regular in-out waveform, while the Grecian is a much fuller and less symmetrical shape. Each has its uses and which one you prefer is a matter of taste. The Roman type can be broken in the middle by a quirk or 'step', thus producing what is known as a 'classic-style' cutter. Ogee cutters may or may not have bearings and the 'Roman' profile often turns up on frame and panel cutters as well.

Back row: from left to right, Grecian, Roman, flat.
Front row: from left to right, Grecian, two Roman, plain.

SPECIALIST CUTTERS

Some of the most useful cutters are perhaps not on the list of what one might call 'basic' cutters. They do deserve mention, so here is a round-up of these more exotic items.

Side-profile cutters

Once upon a time, moulding handrails was the exclusive preserve of the spindle moulder, but not any more. A number of cutter manufacturers have a range of side-moulding cutters, which, allied to their other cutters, give a range of up to nine shape combinations for handrailing. If you fancy making up something a bit different for your home, this could be it.

Drawer pull

Making decent drawer pulls can ordinarily be a nuisance, but again there is a good choice of router cutters that are designed to be used in a number of ways. Often it means canting the workpiece at an angle as it runs across the router table to create the correct profile.

Corian cutters

Nowadays, Corian worktops are fitted in expensive kitchens and bathrooms. There is a whole range of cutters designed specifically for this material, with nylon-sleeved bearings made so they do not mark the material.

Aluminium cutters

There are various burrs and rasps and special spiral cutters for aluminium, designed for the double-glazing industry.

Drill bits

Drilling is not just the preserve of the cordless or mains drill. The router is better equipped to do this job where wood and plastic are concerned. Routers have plenty of power, they run at high speeds, and they cut exactly perpendicular to the worksurface and to a precise depth. Ordinary straight bits do quite a good job, but there are also some special spiral drill bits that are capable of countersinking. They don't cut to a great depth but do have some uses.

Hinge sinkers

Another good idea is the hinge sinker for fitting kitchen-cabinet hinges. Used with a router and fence it is possible to get very accurate drilling without accidentally going through to the front of the door frame. I have done this on-site many times with great success.

Linenfold cutters

An exciting cutter development is the linenfold cutter set from Wealden Cutters. This brings a traditional and very stylized moulding pattern within reach of the average router user. Formerly, this would have been the province of a woodcarver equipped with carving chisels and a set of ancient moulding planes. The set comes as a matched pair of cutters and with proper instructions for making a jig to suit.

Customized cutters

Some cutter suppliers can make a special profile cutter to order, but this is expensive, so don't consider it unless you have a very special requirement that can't be met by a standard cutter.

Back row: from left to right, sash bar (window bar) set, corian, drawer pull, corian.
Front row: from left to right, keyhole, hinge sinker, burr, acrylic, multi-profile.

UNUSUAL STRAIGHT CUTTERS

This group of cutters show how flexible the definition of 'straight' can be. It shows just how diverse router cutters and their uses really are.

Pocket

Pocket cutters are designed for deep grooving, rebating and mortises. They are mostly shank and not much cutter. They also may have recessed shanks to allow machining deep into the wood. The cutting head may have a single flute if it is a smaller diameter or two flute in larger sizes.

Stagger-tooth (mortising)

The stagger-tooth cutter needs to be used carefully. The cutting edges are split into two overlapping sections opposing each other. Thus you get a single flute cutting edge but in two separate sections 180° apart. This gives a rather rough cutting action with good chip clearance in a deep mortise, so a mortise box is essential to keep the router on track. Stagger-tooth cutters are not intended to plunge, so a technique known as 'ramping' is required. Keep the plunge unlocked and move around the jig in a clockwise direction, plunging slightly with each pass, and continue all the way to the bottom of the mortise before doing a final clean-up pass to ensure it is full size and shape all round.

Down shear

Standard straight cutters defy common sense because with a short cutter length and small diameter they strike the wood perpendicular to the feed direction, where a large planer machine can cut more efficiently due to the diameter of the cutterblock and number of blades, in some cases three or four cutters. A shearing cut, attacking at an angle, has a smoother slicing action, which this and the alternative up-down shear cutter are designed to do. It gives a fast cut and crucially a smooth finish on faced boards, eliminating breakout or feathering.

Up-down shear

A similar result except it gives a neat finish on both faces of a board. It has split cutters similar to the stagger-tooth cutter but mounted and ground to give a shear cut not a straight across cut.

Up-cut spiral

CNC machines make great demands on cutters and the cutters can be different in profile because of the tasks they perform given the total control that the CNC head exerts over tooling. However, there are some types that are compatible with hand-held routers, such as spiral cutters. The complex shape means they are made from one solid piece of metal. The carbide version will handle hardwoods and abrasive man-made materials. Up-cut types reduce burning when plunging, while down-cut will help hold workpieces in place on vacuum jigs and additionally gives a clean surface cut. The up-down cut variant gives a clean finish on both faces of hardwood but, unsurprisingly, this is an expensive piece of tooling.

Tapered straight

This profile isn't quite straight but is very close to being a straight cutter. It could easily get overlooked as not belonging to any other category. It is intended for wooden vacuum moulds to aid release. There could also be other uses for a cutter with a subtle taper like this.

Acrylic and other plastics

There are several different patterns of cutter, which depend on the type of plastic that is being machined. Acrylics, in particular, fare better with multiple-flute spiral cutters that have a polished finish to avoid the material melting and congealing in hardened lumps. Acrylic comes in various colours and is used for signs, templates and so on. Note the way static has made the shaving adhere temporarily to the router.

Extra long (honeycomb)

This straight cutter is one to avoid for normal use. It is longer than other cutters and will not withstand the strain of machining wood. It is intended for lightweight man-made honeycomb material that offers limited resistance.

Replaceable blade

There are many different replaceable cutter types; however, the straight variant has many obvious uses. The smaller sizes can be used with handheld machines while the larger cutters are for fixed-head machines. Whether single or two cutter types, the blades can quickly be rotated or exchanged to give new edges at reduced cost and without demounting the cutter.

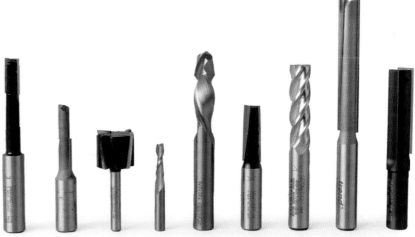

Left to right – pocket, stagger-tooth, tenoning (upshear/downshear example), up spiral, up-down spiral, taper, acrylic and plastics, honeycomb core, replaceable blade.

CHOOSING A STARTER SET OF CUTTERS

Having read all the previous descriptions, you may feel dazed and confused by the diversity of cutter tooling. It is only fair that I try to suggest what priorities you need to consider when selecting cutters. If you are a novice, don't think of buying a big ½in router. Choose a ¼in model, capable of taking an 8mm collet size, with power to match, if this suits your needs. This will narrow your cutter choice straightaway.

Nearly all cutter manufacturers and suppliers produce starter sets that include all the popular items a new user is likely to need. These represent both a good choice and value for money, because the cost of a set in a box or case is lower than that of buying the cutters individually. There are many cheap cutter sets on the market, but I would recommend paying more money for a respected brand; however, even well-known manufacturers now resort to buying in cheap imports for their starter sets.

Since the cutters are fundamental to routing, it makes good sense to equip yourself properly. Once bought, these cutters will repay the initial outlay by returning good service for a long time if you look after them properly.

A set will usually consist of the following:

- two straight cutters
- a bearing-guided trimmer
- a rebater
- a V-groove
- a corebox
- a cove
- a dovetail
- an ogee
- two roundover/ovolos
- a chamfer cutter

There are variations on this, including different cutter sizes or perhaps several of one type, but this initial group will cover most circumstances if used with a little imagination. The inclusion of a dovetail cutter always seems a bit strange as most people won't use it, and if you do need one it has to match the dovetail jig you are going to work with. Obviously, the really big and exotic profiles tend to come in ½in-shank size, but you have to start somewhere and learn about routing and cutters in the process.

A well-specified ¼-in shank starter set.

CHOOSING AN ADVANCED SET OF CUTTERS

My own taste in cutters tends to include the following, which you may find a useful guide to choosing cutters. These are all TCT cutters. Some are only available in 1/2in-shank size and are additional to any starter set you may have:

- a variety of straight cutters, from 1/16in (2mm) and 3/16in (4mm) (for biscuit slotting in mid-panel positions), through to 3/8in (9.5mm) with 1/4in shank for general work, right up to a long 3/4in- (19mm-) diameter cutter with a good spread of different sizes in between
- a 1/4in (5mm) two-flute straight cutter for drilling stud holes to support shelves
- a 1 3/8in (35mm) hinge sinker for quick and precise drilling of hinge holes in kitchen cabinets
- long stagger-tooth or pocket cutters for mortising in 3/8, 1/2, 5/8in and 3/4in (9.5, 12.7, 16 and 19mm) diameters
- a classical-pattern profile-and-scribe set. These are good for cabinet doors or room panelling
- an ogee or bevel pattern profile-and-scribe set (excellent for kitchen and other doors)
- a large bevel panel-raiser for making door panels
- a 'regency' panel-raiser for a more sophisticated look to door panels
- roundover/ovolo cutters in 1/8, 1/2in (3.2, 12.7mm) and larger (the smallest of these gives a tiny but distinctive finish to the edge of a modern piece of furniture)
- cove cutters in 1/2in (12.7mm) and 5/8in (16mm) or larger sizes (useful for making built-up cornice, among other things)
- corebox cutters, 3/8 and 5/8in (9.5 and 16mm) (the 3/8in/9.5mm) is ideal for creating flutings to give a mock column effect on a piece of furniture)
- 1/4 and 3/8in (6.4 and 9.5mm) corner bead cutters for door meetings in order to disguise discrepancies between doors, and for adding detail. This is also good for detailing the corners of table legs, and so on
- a biscuit cutter set (this is ideal, even with a small router, as a substitute for a jointing machine. It won't do everything the jointer can but it will make normal edge-to-edge or corner joints and, unusually, it will make joints on curves and in other difficult situations)
- hinge mortise cutter in 1/2 and 5/8in (12.7 and 16mm) sizes (these make a neat, quick job of setting-in brass butt hinges and will do other shallow surface work).

Clearly, no beginner or even many advanced router users are going to have all these cutters or even the need to use them. But they do show what a heavy-duty kit could consist of and suggest the wide variety of work it is possible to undertake with a router.

A selection of advanced cutters.

GALLERY OF CUTTERS

There are lots of cutters from a variety of brands to choose from; here is a selection of just a few to give you an idea of what is available. It is worth collecting tool dealers' and cutter manufacturers' catalogues so you can make an informed selection based on quality, cost and design.

Clico (UK)

Carbitool (Aus)

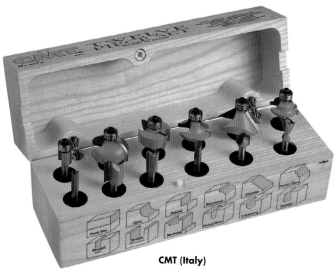

CMT (Italy)

All the above: Freud (US)

Oldham Viper (US)

Trend Trade (UK)

Wealden (UK)

Makita professional cutters

Trend dovetail key set

Infinity multi-bearing rebate set

CHAPTER 5

BASIC HANDHELD OPERATIONS

The first thing anyone new to routing will do (and many old hands too) is to use the router freehand. There is nothing wrong with this, but you need to understand how to have proper control over the machine to achieve the best results. You must always use some form of guidance, or disaster may ensue.

GUIDING THE ROUTER WITH A STRAIGHT FENCE

For most operations, the router needs proper directional guidance. The most common method is to use the straight fence. Routers are always supplied with such a device and there are two holes machined into the base of the router to take the fence rods. These allow you to fix the fence at a certain distance from the cutter.

Adjusting the fence
Fences vary in sophistication, from simple pressed steel to neat alloy castings or even tough moulded plastics. With the basic kind, adjusting the fence is just a matter of slacking off the locking knobs on the router base and pushing the fence in or out

Using a ruler and a straightedge to adjust the fence on the router.

and then relocking. It has long been recognized that this is not ideal – quite fine adjustments are sometimes needed, especially for critically accurate work. Router manufacturers have come up with various solutions, but they don't all work as well as intended. Before buying a router that has a fine fence adjustment, it is worth testing to see how well it works. It should be just a matter of unlocking one knob and twisting another so that the fence can move smoothly in or out. In practice, this degree of adjustment, although useful, is not always needed; a gentle tap or nudge of the fence will often get it into the correct position for locking.

Adjusting the plastic facings on the fence.

Edge-machining, pulling the router, thus giving good control.

Usually a fence will have adjustable plastic facings that can be moved as near to the cutter as it will allow for a nearly continuous surface. This makes for better support and resultant accuracy.

USING THE FENCE

The normal procedure for machining is to set the fence-to-cutter distance first and only then to set the cutter depth.

When machining, it is necessary to apply a little side pressure to keep the fence firmly against the side of the work. Any lumps or bumps on the side of a workpiece will push the fence off course and spoil the cut. Get into the habit of pulling the router towards you, because a pushing action often causes the machine to wander in the direction of the fence.

It is fairly safe to cut the far side of a wide slot (i.e. the side furthest from the fence); if you go off course you will only be cutting into wood you won't be needing anyway. The near side is more critical, because any deviation will mark the wood that you wish to keep. Sometimes there are ways around this problem.

Use a drill shank to give an exact depth setting. More sophisticated machines have more accurate geared, micrometer-type depth stops.

Machining the far side of a recess to avoid accidentally cutting into good material.

Using fence rods

The more expensive routers have fence rods that are separate from the fence. This makes it possible to work near to projecting surfaces that the rods might otherwise catch unless they are adjusted out of the way. Another advantage is that for working on narrow workpieces it is possible to buy another fence, which fits onto the other end of the rods. With these tight against the workpiece, and with the cutter in the correct position, there is no danger of the router wandering off – it is rather like a train sitting on rails.

If the fence rods are fixed, they tend to be short. Therefore there is a limit to the distance the cutter can be from the edge of the work. In this case, other means of guidance become necessary (see p. 83).

Supporting the fence and the router base

One error that everyone makes, including professionals, is not allowing enough extra material at the ends of a workpiece to give support to the fence and the router base. Because of this, nasty dips or 'dig ins' result that mar the work. Make sure that your workpiece is longer than it needs to be even if this seems wasteful. You can usually trim it down with a jigsaw or circular saw, or even the router itself, which makes an excellent board trimmer.

When a component needs to be machined at its finished size, it may be possible to fix a longer piece of material alongside the workpiece. This will at least give support to either the fence or the router base. The only problem that remains then is providing the rest of the support by holding the router very carefully. A better solution is to build or buy a router table (see p. 99 [Chapter 7]). This is an excellent way to give proper support during handheld operations when circumstances make things difficult.

Working with two fences.

An overlong workpiece will give the router base more support and help to keep it level.

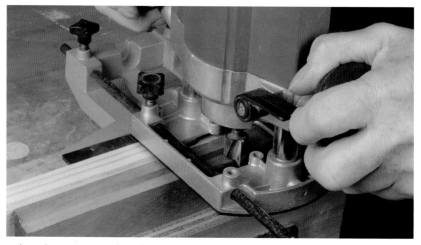

A clamped-on extension strip for rock-steady routing. If this strip is placed next to the fence it also prevents the fence from waggling about at the end of the cut.

ROUTING ON NARROW EDGES

It is quite possible to use the router on narrow edges, but a steady hand and a good eye are required to ensure that the router is sitting squarely on the edge. It may be that the fence is on the inside of a carcass, in which case the fence will hit the inside corner of the carcass and prevent the cutter from reaching the corner. The best plan is to think through any project you have in mind and try to do as much routing as possible before you assemble it. It is much easier to work on individual components than struggling with something that has already been put together. (See the Projects sections, pp. 141–245. These give the correct machining order and will help you to understand the need for planning and organizing your work methods.)

EDGE PLANING

It is possible to use a router and a straight fence for planing the edges of short workpieces. Trend Ltd produces such a device for Trend and other routers with similar fence fittings, but it is possible to improvise. Normally a big planer machine has surface tables that are at least 3ft 3in (1m) long, ensuring that edges are true over some distance. The router fence is not very long, so don't expect a high degree of accuracy, especially with long pieces of wood. Still, it is another way of getting the router to prepare your materials as well as do the mouldings.

To turn your fence into a planer fence, buy a short roll of melamine edging tape from a do-it-yourself store and iron it down onto the section of fence on the 'outfeed' side of the cutter (use an old iron). To identify the outfeed side, fit the fence and, with a cutter in place, choose the fence section that the cutter will rotate away from when in operation. This is the correct fence section, because as the workpiece moves past the cutter, it will take off a given thickness of wood in the way that a planer does.

The workpiece needs support equivalent to the thickness of the material that is machined off, which is where the tape comes in. Apply one or two thicknesses of tape to the fence edge and let the glue harden. Too many layers will result in too much being taken off in one go. Now, using the edge of a steel rule pressed flat against the taped outfeed fence section, adjust the fence so that the cutter is flush with the tape. Before planing, ensure that the edge of the wood is reasonably well sawn so that it is fairly straight to start with, then run the router along the edge to give a clean finish. Check the trueness of the edge with a steel rule or even by eye. If it is not straight, apply the router to the offending section only to try to level that part, then run the router along the entire edge to get a neat and true edge.

A fence to which iron-on edging tape has been added on the outfeed section.

BEARING-GUIDED CUTTERS

Many of today's cutters come with one or more bearings. This allows you to work along awkwardly shaped edges rather than just straight edges. Cutters sometimes come with a guide pin (or pilot). These can be useful because they can get into tight corners, unlike many bearings, but should be avoided even if the cost seems more attractive. The guide pin can dent the workpiece and the friction it creates can burn it. Cutters that come with more than one size of bearing give different effects and increase the cutter's versatility for little extra cost.

Some cutters don't need bearings fitted because the bearing would simply get in the way of operations (such as plunge cutting with a straight cutter). Others, like the rebater, cannot function without a bearing. So any set of cutters needs to have a mixture of both in order to satisfy the various machining needs. Different results can be obtained by using the same cutter with different-sized bearings

The bearing is located at the end of the cutter spindle. It is held on with a small Allen screw and a washer. It is possible to cut without the bearing in place. This can be useful when the bearing is either too large or too small for the job in hand, but you need to use a straight fence or a router table so that the cutter remains guided.

Bearing-guided cutters are fitted with bottom- or top-mounted bearings. If these cutters are resharpened, it follows that the bearing will be slightly too large once the cutting edges have been ground down. It is not usual practice to grind the bearings to match, so the user just has to accept that there is discrepancy in size.

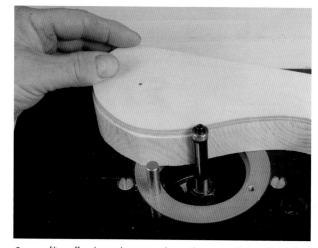

A bearing-guided cutter is easy to use as an alternative to a fence.

A large panel raiser fitted with a tongue cutter shaping the top of an arabesque-style door panel.

Copy profiling off a ply template using a bottom-bearing-guided profiling cutter.

Router diversity: different results obtained by using the same cutter with different-sized bearings.

USING A STRAIGHTEDGE AND GUIDE RAIL

There are times when neither a fence nor a bearing-guided cutter will do. If you want to make a long straight cut or a cut well away from the edge of a workpiece, or true up an uneven board edge or even cut it to length, then the straightedge is the way to go.

The most basic method is to use a ¾in (18mm)-thick piece of wood or strip of MDF about 5in (125mm) wide. It should be cut carefully; you need it to be dead straight and true, because any bend or kink makes it pretty useless.

The featheredge

The alternative is to use a plasterer's featheredge. Made of extruded aluminium, with a tapered edge, this is handy for drawing out the size and shape of the piece you wish to cut. The other edge is vertical – it is this one that the router runs against to make the cut. The featheredge comes in different lengths. I have found the 8ft (2.4m) version to be most useful, as it matches standard manufactured board sizes, making easy work of cutting and moulding ply, chipboard and MDF.

Using a straightedge

The technique for using any straightedge involves working out the distance between the edge of the cutter and the flat running edge of the router base. Some routers have circular bases; avoid rotating the router as you move it along the straightedge in case the base isn't concentric with the cutter axis. Once you know the cutter-to-base edge offset (and it varies according to the cutter that you have fitted), it is easy to mark that distance back from the original size that you have marked out on the board. If you choose to make your own straightedge from a strip of board, you could fit a couple of handles onto it to make it easy to pick up. You could also mark onto it

Using a plasterer's featheredge. The strip of tape is marked with a reminder of the offset required when using a standard cutter.

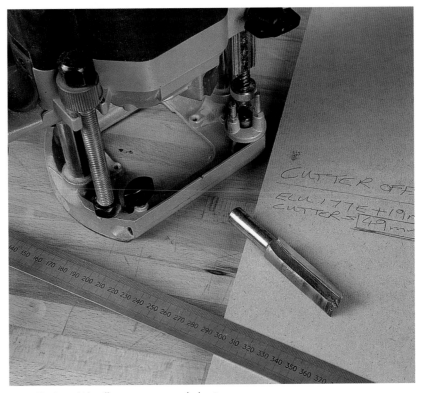

A straightedge with the offset measurement marked on it.

the offset measurements relating to the cutters you intend to use. Of course, if you stick to just one cutter diameter, you won't get in a muddle.

Clamp the strip down in the correct position and run the router along it until the cut is done. To clamp the straightedge, it is useful to have a quick one-handed method of holding the straightedge on the work. I have found that 'quick' clamps are excellent for locking a straightedge in place quickly. G-cramps, which take a bit longer to tighten or loosen, are fiddly but dependable.

This is an accurate way of working, especially when you get used to measuring the distance between the cutter and the edge of the router base. Care is needed when pulling the router along the straightedge over a long distance because it is easy for the router to wander off course. If you ensure that you are cutting into the waste piece, that isn't such a worry. Using this method, it is possible to make lots of cuts anywhere on a board.

Generally, manufactured boards are sawn square, which makes crosscutting easier. However, you can verify that a board is square by measuring and marking a square, starting at one board end and spanning the entire width. Once this is done, accurately measure across the diagonals – the readings should be identical. If they aren't, then adjust your crosscut marking out accordingly.

Checking that a board is square. Masking tape has been used here to emphasize the pencil line.

■ GUIDE RAILS

Some router manufacturers have devised their own guide rail systems that are better, though more expensive, than the methods previously described. Guide rails come in sections (often about 4ft/1.2m long), which can be joined together to make longer rails. Festool, Bosch and DeWalt are just three of the companies that use this system. There is a small step in the aluminium extrusion that forms the rail. An adapter fits onto the fence rails and sits over this step. This keeps the router running true from one end of the rail to the other. This system is also shared with other tools in the manufacturer's range, such as circular saws, and gives reliable results in the workshop or on-site.

A guide rail in use.

ROLLER GUIDES

There are occasions when a normal fence or a bearing-guided cutter cannot be used. An example might be a table base with lots of curves that needs a top to match that will overhang by the same amount all round. Shaping such a top without a template would be a problem. In practice, you need to remove most of the waste first, leaving about 1/16–1/8in (2–3mm) to be trimmed off.

To complete the final shaping, you need to fit a roller guide to your router. This is, as the name suggests, a roller that follows an existing surface so that the cutter follows the same path. The roller is mounted onto an adjustable guide assembly that hangs down below the base of the router. It is often fitted to

the fence on cheaper models, although on professional machines it may have a separate means of attachment. The roller guide can be moved up and down and towards or away from the cutter axis.

As with all router operations, it is as well to make a test cut on spare material after you have set the roller: however careful you are, it is difficult to get any setting spot on. It is never a good idea to do a test cut on your actual workpiece; it is easy to take too much material away. For instance, let's suppose we are shaping a top on a table overhanging by 3/8in (10mm). The roller needs to be positioned 3/8in (10mm) closer to the table than the

cutter itself. It is sensible to raise the roller so that it is as close to the tabletop as possible, thus ensuring that the top follows the table shape as closely as possible. Any lower and there may be a variation, especially if the base is flared in shape.

When following a shape with a roller guide, it is important to keep the guide bracket at 90° to the face of the workpiece. Unlike an ordinary fence, there is nothing to stop the router swinging about the axis of the roller, giving a rather irregular cut that does not exactly mirror that of the original workpiece. Basically that is all there is to this gadget. You won't need it much, but it is very handy when you do.

A roller guide in use.

ROUTER CARVING

The router may not seem a natural replacement for what is essentially a hand skill, but it has its uses even in this area. For small work, when you want to add some detail to an otherwise plain item, for instance, you can try using a router (try it out on a scrap piece first). Use only the tip of a V-cutter or a straight cutter with a very small diameter. Larger cutters or passes will be erratic and tend to move the router in unexpected directions. Mark out a simple design, set the required plunge depth, and go to work. This kind of work requires patience and the ability to follow a line carefully. As the scale of work is so small, it may be better and quite safe to hold the edge of the router base instead of the handles and gently push it back and forth working along each line until it is neat.

Carving freehand: note that the base is held for better control. This is an exception to the no 'backfeeding' rule: the point-only contact allows the operator kickback-free fine machining.

TRIMMING LAMINATES AND PROFILES

Nowadays, in the age of the post-formed kitchen worktop, it isn't quite so necessary to use stick-on laminates that subsequently need trimming. The main uses for laminates today are shopfitting, reception areas, airport check-in areas, bank counters and caravan interiors, which tend to be the domain of the professional woodworker. Nevertheless, there are still times when laminate and contact adhesive are the only solution to a problem. At other times, you may find yourself with veneered boards and other materials that require neat trimming. A range of trimmers is available for this. There are also straight trimmers for flushing off the solid lippings that are added to the edges of carcasses and worktops.

These cutters are quite simple to use. The main thing is to avoid trying to trim off too much waste material in the first place. No matter how thick the material, it should not project more than about ⅛in (3mm). More than this and the cutter will find it hard to cope. The material, whether solid wood or laminate, can break up and leave a ragged edge even after the cutter has trimmed the material flush. If a bearing-guided trimmer is used, the bearing runs against the finished edge of the board while the blade cuts the projecting laminate off.

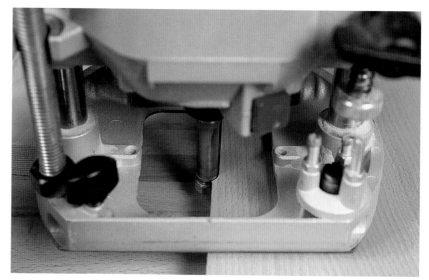

Machining an acceptable amount of laminate overhang.

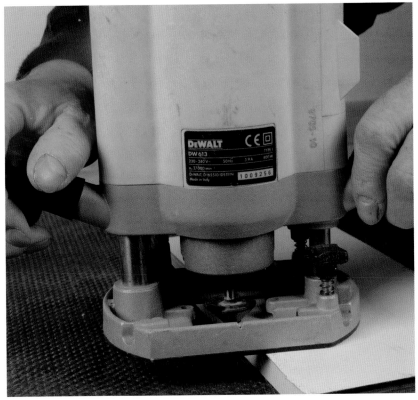

Using a bevel cutter to trim laminate so the finished profile has a slight bevel edge.

There are bevel trimmers that do a little more than that: they will put a tiny bevel on the top edge, or the bottom as well in the case of a twin-bladed type. This is often better than a straight trimmer, because a dead-square edge to a worktop is uncomfortable to the touch.

If you need to trim an inside shape, such as a hole in a worktop to take a sink, then the pencil-slim pierce-and-trim cutter is a neat answer. This uses the shank top and bottom as a pilot and it can work right into an internal corner. It comes in single- or two-bladed types for trimming on the top alone, or on the underside at the same time. At the bottom, it has a cutter to help it pierce through the laminate sheet. The bearings can get gummed up with glue and need regular cleaning – they may have glue shields fitted to reduce this problem.

A pierce and trim cutter can be plunged through the unsupported laminate run against the inside edge of the underlying cutout, even though it has no bearing for guidance.

★ WORKING TIP

If you are trimming an overhanging laminate or veneer, the chances are there will be glue deposits on the board edge underneath. The cutter bearing will run against this and produce a very uneven result. Try and contain the glue to the meeting surfaces and if necessary wipe off surplus while it is still wet. This will also reduce the amount of glue gumming up the bearing.

Using skis and a bottom trim cutter to clean the inset strip of wood flush with the surrounding surface.

■ THE LAMINATE TRIMMER

Although it sounds like a cutter, this is in fact a small router for trimming. It will accept most small cutters and will take a roller guide and possibly even a small straight fence. It is a fairly compact machine, usually tall and slim in shape with 550–600 watts of power. If a lot of small-edge work is required, this may be a suitable solution. While the laminate trimmer is not a proper substitute for a small router, it is very useful in many circumstances.

The DeWalt 670 laminate trimmer is a compact, versatile unit.

Lastly, the flat, bottom-type trimmer is ideal for flush-trimming solid strips inlaid into a larger surface, or for cleaning up background areas when doing relief carving. In both cases you would need to use 'skis'. These are made for several types of well-known router, but it is possible to make your own. The skis lift the router so that the base can pass over any wood that stands proud of the surface. The skis slide on a level surface either side of the working area. The cutter needs to be carefully adjusted downwards until it neatly skims the surface. The correct type of cutter has three blade 'wings' and bevelled or rounded corners to stop it digging in. Ideally, a fine depth-adjuster needs to be fitted to the router for precision setting, although cheap models may not accept one.

USING CUTTERS FOR FREEHAND WORK

Some cutters look so large and fearsome that using them for freehand work just doesn't feel right, but there must be a more rational way of deciding what is safe and wise to use.

Catalogues usually give excellent guidance on what cutters must be used in a router table rather than freehand. Most cutter manufacturers and suppliers mark those that shouldn't be used freehand with a warning statement and sometimes a symbol, too. The ones you shouldn't use in this way tend to be the largest sizes, because the sheer mass of spinning metal and the force involved when they strike the wood makes them much more dangerous than smaller versions of the same cutter.

A glance at the catalogues shows straightaway that most cutters can be used freehand, even if it isn't always a good idea. The dangerous cutters are mainly the ones with complicated moulding profiles. If the router moves around during the cutting, they can damage the wood badly. As a beginner, with a small router capable of using just ¼in shanked cutters, the choice is made for you, because cutters of this size are not big enough to be a risk. Perhaps what is more important is not whether you should be doing everything freehand, but whether it wouldn't in fact be better

Above, top: a difficult moulding tackled freehand. Below: the same moulding done on a table.

The small cutter shown on the left can be used freehand, but not the larger one shown on the right.

to use a table. The router table offers much more control and greater safety. With hold-downs and a good view of the work, it is possible to achieve a much better and more precise finish. All basic operations with straight cutters and simple moulding shapes, like the roundover, cove or chamfer cutter, work well freehand. More complicated shapes, especially when they are built up cut after cut, need to be made with a router table (see p. 98 [Chapter 7] for more information on using router tables).

CHAPTER 6

JIGS AND TEMPLATES

Here we look at making and using jigs and templates. Both bearing-guided and ordinary cutters can be used, depending on the work.

USING JIGS AND TEMPLATES

Technically, a jig is a device that locates parts, and the machine, in order to make accurate and repetitious operations possible. Examples would be machining cutouts for hinges and mortising table legs. In these cases, existing components have to be held and located precisely so that the machining is accurate and all components will match. Jigs are usually made from hard and dense materials such as MDF or Tufnol, and can be reused many times.

A template is similar. It can be made of MDF or plywood and can be used to create a specific shape, such as the swept shape of a rear chair leg, or the outline, windows and doors of a dolls' house. In this case, however, the material is unshaped, except in thickness; machining it will confer a proper shape upon it.

You would usually start by creating a shape with a template and then machining any specific areas on that shape with a jig.

For any jig or template to work, you need some means of guiding the router and therefore the cutter. Bearing-guided cutters can be used, although it is customary to use guide bushes fitted to the base of the router. The guide bush will be larger than the cutter, so you need to calculate the difference between the two before marking out a jig – the holes will need to be bigger than the actual finished size. Expensive machines take guide bushes in a variety of sizes, enabling the operator to use a variety of cutter sizes. It is worth adding that it is difficult to guarantee absolute guide bush concentricity with the cutter axis on cheap machines. This can prevent you achieving

an accurate result. It is worth checking your guide-bush set-up with a steel ruler before you start work. Here are a number of templates and jigs that may be useful.

A typical hinge jig.

TEMPLATES FOR FREEHAND WORK

It is possible to combine a jig and a template on one piece of work. A good example is the front panel of a dolls' house. This has both an outline, which requires a template, and various window and door piercings, which need a jig. Dolls' houses are popular and making them can be interesting – and it's easy with a router and a bit of common sense.

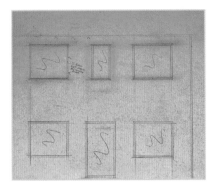

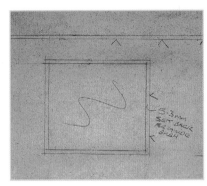

1 Draw the shape onto the thin board that will be used as the template. Get the outline shape right and add the windows and door.

2 Choose a cutter and the guide bush that matches it. A cutter with a reasonably small diameter is sensible, because it will leave the corners of windows and so on with just a small, rounded shape. For neat, fairly square corners, a 6.4mm-diameter (¼in) cutter is best. Measure the difference in both external diameters (vernier callipers are useful here) and calculate the difference. Let's suppose the guide bush is 17mm (1 ¹⁄₁₆in) diameter and the cutter is 6.4mm (¼in). Subtracting 6.4 (¼) from 17 (1 ¹⁄₁₆) gives you 10.6 (⁷⁄₁₆). Dividing this by two, because the difference is split between both sides of the cutter, will give you 5.3 (³⁄₁₆). Now mark back from your existing drawn lines by 5.3mm (³⁄₁₆), thus making all openings larger and the outline smaller all round (it is easier to round down this figure to 5mm).

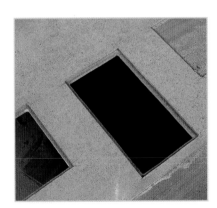

3 Take your router, minus the guide bush, and use the 6.4mm (¼in) cutter and a clamped-on straightedge to shape the template following the new set of lines. This will take a while; take care to avoid overrunning at the start and finish of each cut where they meet at the corners.

4 Use some panel pins to fix the template to the intended workpiece. This might seem like a lot of effort, but if you want to produce even limited quantities of the same design, then this is the way to do it.

5 Having machined the front panel, the sides and back present no problem. Often the back is just plain, so it may be practical to use the front template but miss out the windows and door. The ends, or sides, of the house could be identical. This repetitive work can be applied to other parts of a dolls' house, such as stairwells and internal walls, roof shapes and chimneys.

A TEMPLATE FOR A NAME PLAQUE

Demonstrated on this page is the method of making a house name plaque. It will have a bevelled profile.

The plaque is rectangular and could be cut on a table saw or with a jigsaw and then cleaned up with the template and cutter. This operation needs to be done on a router table.

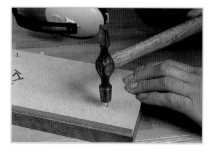

1 Cut out the template accurately with the router. Make sure that you make a proper rectangular shape by using a set square. Cramp on a straightedge in order to make a neat cut with a straight cutter. As the template is only ¼–⅜in (6–9mm)-thick MDF, this can be done in just a couple of passes. Repeat this cut-through operation until you have done all four sides and the template drops out of the board. Pin the template to the reverse of the workpiece, which should be ⅛in (2–3mm) bigger all round.

2 Fit the router in the table and use a straight cutter with a bottom-mounted bearing (actually at the top when the router is inverted). Wind it up through the hole until the workpiece and template are next to the cutter. Adjust the router height until the bearing is just slightly against the cutter.

3 Note that a Perspex guard should be fitted over the cutter. You will also need a lead-in point to safely support the work as it approaches the cutter – not to do so will result in an alarming kickback as the workpiece catches the cutter and is chucked aside.

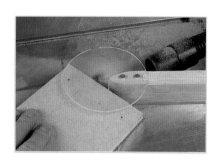

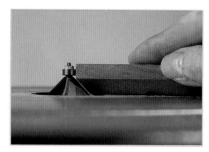

4 Start the cut along one long-grain edge, to gain confidence. The wood goes to the left of the cutter, in front of it and against the rotation of the cutter. Push at a firm, even rate, and, by carefully changing your grip, continue the cut all round the edges. Having done this exercise once and got used to this kind of machining, make a habit of doing the cross-grain passes first. The reason is that tearout may occur and you need some excess material on the long-grain edges so that any torn wood can be machined away when you make the long-grain passes.

5 You should now have a neat rectangular piece of wood that needs a bevel to complete it. To do this, fit a chamfer cutter in the router and remove the template from the wood. Raise the cutter till the bearing runs along the last third of the edge of the workpiece. Now start cutting as before and run all around the edge. The result should be a neat bevel effect on what will be the outer face of the name plaque.

6 You can now add readymade letters to this name plaque, or try your hand at router carving with a V-point cutter (see p. 86 [Chapter 5]). Obviously, you can vary the amount of bevel by raising or lowering the cutter, as long as the bearing is still in contact with the work-piece. More complex and irregular shapes can be created and, as long as the template is well made, the cutter must follow it. Here the letters of the finished house name plaque are emphasized with black lacquer.

WORKTOP JOINTING

Building and fitting a new kitchen is a pretty common activity, and jigs and templates are natural for this kind of work. I'll start with worktop jointing. The standard type of kitchen worktop is postformed laminate with a 1¼–1½in (30–40mm) chipboard core. There are other materials of course, such as solid hardwood, granite and Corian, which is an expensive manmade worksurface material. Post-formed laminate has a rounded front edge, which means that any joint, other than in a straight run, needs to be a special offset joint like a dogleg. Professional kitchen fitters use special Tufnol or aluminium jigs; these make both halves of the joint and the recesses underneath, which take the special worktop bolts that pull the joint together. Not surprisingly, such a jig is expensive, so for the occasional user here must be a simpler answer.

The Combi Jig1001 is one of a range from Trend designed to meet all the needs of kitchen-fitters and tradesmen.

1 MDF is cheap and is ideal for this job. In fact, if you are going to be a serious router user, it is a good idea to keep some MDF in stock at all times. You will need ¼–½in (6–12mm)-thick MDF for jigs and templates, with thicker board for actual projects. Accurate drawing is necessary, so use a long steel rule and a sharp pencil to mark out your jig on some ⅜in (9.5mm) MDF. This one-part jig is for use with a guide bush and requires a big router. The thickness of cut and the stress imposed on a ¼in router and cutter would be too much and the cutters available are just too short. The small openings are for worktop bolt recesses and are made after the joint is cut.

2 To use the jig, push it against the worktop so that it is in line with the worktop edge. Note that one half of the joint is made from above and the other from below, because the cutter must always start at the front edge of the worktop. If you were to cut from the back towards the front, the laminate would rip off the front edge and ruin it – so one pass must be done with the worktop inverted.

3 Fix a 2 x 1in (25 x 50mm) batten all round the walls at the height of the units, which should have been levelled already. This batten will carry the back edge of the worktop. It will be fixed to the batten with angled steel plates or nylon blocks. When fitting the worktop, ensure that you have enough to do the job.

Decide where the joints should be – this may be dictated by the position of appliances or walls. Mark and cut your first section to fit between walls and so on. Try to arrange things so that you first make the joint half that is recessed into the front edge of a worktop. Then sit that half of the joint on top of the other worktop section in situ and mark along the edge of the joint onto the uncut worktop. This should give an accurate line for the second cut. Now fit the jig again and cut (in a number of passes) to the full depth, put the resulting joint together, and check the fit. Make the rest of the connecting joints and then the bolt recesses. These allow the bolts to fit neatly so that they can be tightened with a C spanner.

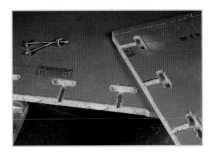

4 Use an arbor and groover to biscuit joint the edge (see slotters, p. 68 Chapter 4]). This prevents any warping or misalignment between worktop sections. The postform joint can be used with hardwood worktops, although the amount of dogleg can be reduced, because any roundover on the edge is normally much smaller than that on laminate tops.

PRECISION DRILLING

The router is a better drill than any conventional drill, within its own limited capacity. This aspect of the router has perhaps not been exploited much by cutter manufacturers, except on full industrial machinery. What makes it so good is its ability to drill straight and true every time; it is sometimes very difficult to aim a power drill straight unless it is mounted in a stand. Also, drill bits tend to wander and chip the surrounding surface unless they are proper bradpoint drill bits or Black & Decker 'Bullet' bits.

Drill bits for the router come in a limited number of sizes and they often double as countersinks or counterbores. They are extremely useful and make accurate repetitious work possible. For limited use and for shallow drillings, it is possible to use ordinary straight router bits, such as the ³⁄₁₆in (5mm) size for shelf studs. The disadvantage is that they heat up and collect resin, although each hole is drilled so quickly that this isn't too much of a problem.

To take advantage of this facility, you need to do one of two things. First, you can mark up a piece of thin, clear plastic with crosshairs, such as are found in a telescopic sight of a rifle.

Attach that to the base of the router with double-sided tape. Then plunge the intended cutter through the plastic and you are ready to drill. You can stick some abrasive paper to the base (not over the visible plastic, of course) to act as a grip. The router will then stay put while it drills. Set the router at its lowest speed to prevent burning. The other method is to make a purpose-built jig that accepts a guide bush where each hole is to be drilled. This would be suitable for things like a series of cabinet shelf-supports, or for mounting hinges on the carcass of a kitchen cabinet. This will be more precise than the first method, but may do only one sort of job. Each jig will have to be made to suit your own circumstances, though certain components don't change in size. Kitchen hinges need a 1³⁄₈in (35mm) hole, while shelf studs need a ³⁄₁₆in (5mm) hole. However, the type of hinge and backing plate – these can be separate and of different thicknesses – will determine the exact positioning. The thickness of the carcass also affects this, as does whether a hinge is on an outer panel or a centre panel. In the latter, a slightly cranked hinge is needed.

From left to right: a counterbore cutter, its matching plug cutter, and two router drills.

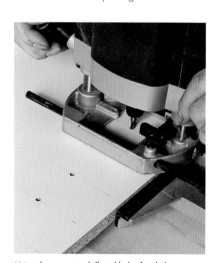

Using the router to drill stud holes for shelves.

A router with crosshair sights.

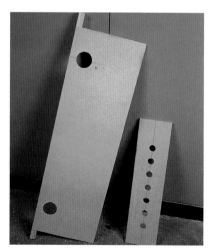

Hinge and shelf stud jigs for kitchen cabinet fittings. Note that the hinge is done with a small cutter and a guide bush to open up a hole with a large diameter.

LOCK AND HINGE JIGS

First, we'll consider a simple hinge jig. You can decide what size of hinge you wish to fit. It might be a large hinge for the door to a room, or a much smaller one for a cabinet: the principle remains the same.

To make small jigs like this, you can use a router, straight cutter and fence to cut out the shape for the guide bush to follow. Inevitably, with a small jig, there may be some tidying up to do, so one or two round and flat files are handy for neatening the internal edges. Rounded corners on the jig are not a problem, because the guide bush is round anyway, just as long as the corners of the jig have the same or smaller radii than that of the guide bush (or even square). Once made, such a simple jig can be used time and again. Several of these jigs will cater for all the usual sizes and give a neat and predictable result. A key feature is leaving enough of a 'wing' at each end so that the jig can be clamped in place properly, and enough running surface on top, so that the router sits properly.

You also need a location mark so that the jig will always be accurately positioned no matter where the hinge is to be placed. The sensible place is in the centre of the jig, this being also the centre of the hinge. An alternative is to make the jig exactly symmetrical so that you can set it to a line using the end of the jig.

Whatever you do, make sure that the guide marks are made on the doors and carcass by striking the pencil across both at the same time. The result is marks that can be relied on to be accurate when using the jig. If you attempt to mark the components separately and away from each other by just using a rule, you are guaranteed to have hinges that will not line up, thus ruining the whole idea of the jig. In order to set the correct cut depth for the hinge, a little experimentation is necessary.

A hinge jig.

Using the router with the hinge jig in place.

If you are setting one half of the hinge into the frame and the other half of it into the door, then start by placing the narrowest part of the opened hinge under the depth stop rod of the router with the cutter at rest on the workpiece. Then lower the rod and trap the hinge at its thinnest point between the rod and the revolving turret. Lock the depth stop, thus giving a set depth for each half of the hinge 'joint'. Another way is to fit it to the door only, in which case you put a closed hinge under the depth stop

rod. Obviously, the fit of the door in the frame affects the tightness of the fit on the opposite side to the hinge – it might leave a big gap or nothing at all. Don't set the hinges in too deep; it isn't necessary and it will pull the door tight against the frame so that it will not shut properly. If this does arise, the only way to deal with it is to fit some packing, such as paper or bits of veneer, under the hinge in order to push the door away from the frame.

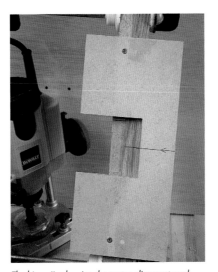

The hinge jig showing the centre-alignment mark.

The hinge trapped under the depth rod at its thinnest part.

LOCK MORTISES

Cutting lock mortises by machine is a lot quicker and easier with a router than it is by hand. Jigs for such a job could range from one designed to set in a shallow cabinet-door lock, which fits on the reverse of a door, to the more typical situation of a lock for a standard room door. The latter stretches the router to its limit in terms of cutter capacity. For a start, it needs a ½in router and a very long, strong, straight cutter specially designed for this kind of operation. Not only does the cutter need to plunge deep in order to make an adequate mortise, but it also needs to be able to clear away a lot of coarse chippings to prevent the socket becoming too congested. If this happens, the cutting rate will slow down and the cutter will overheat.

Currently, the maximum cutter size for this application has a cutting edge about 2in (50mm) or slightly longer, and a diameter of ⅝in (16mm) with a staggered tooth or standard blade configuration. By careful adjustment of the amount of shank in the collet, it is possible to obtain a cut depth of 2¾in (70mm), which will cover shallower mortise lock applications.

Pocket cutters (left) and Stagger-tooth (right). When deep mortising, the extended shank on the pocket cutter enters the hole.

Deepening the hole with a chisel.

Deeper sockets will need to be cleared by chisel and mallet to the right depth, although at least a lot of the work has already been done. To carry out lock mortising, it is possible to use a router with two fences fitted on one set of rods. The disadvantage is that the router moves about on the edge of the door and can't cut an accurate socket parallel to the front and back surfaces of it. It is better to make a jig that sits on

the door and can be clamped in place. As with the hinge jig, make a centre mark that will line up to a pencil mark on the door. Use a guide bush as before, and set it so it does not project through the thickness of the jig material. Although the jig is just ¼in (6mm) thick, it will reduce the possible plunge depth by that amount. A stagger-tooth cutter will give you a bumpy ride, but a quick one. Technically, this isn't a plunge-type cutter, because it doesn't have a bottom cutting part. However, my own experience is that you can make a series of gradual sloping cuts (known as ramping) down to the final depth and then lock the router at full depth and run round in order to smooth the sides of the hole. Note that you will need to make each pass in a clockwise direction, so that the cutter slices into the wood. Having made the mortise, it is usually necessary to square up the corners with a chisel for the lock to fit properly (unless you make the mortise slightly longer).

This isn't the end of the story, of course, because you still have to make a recess for the faceplate and holes for the handle shaft and key. It is best to make a second jig for the

The cabinet lock set in. A chisel is needed to square out the corners of the recess cut by the router.

Making a trial cut for the lock face, using a jig. A separate jig will be needed to cut the deep mortise.

A jig for the handle bar and keyway.

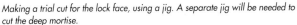

faceplate recessing; this allows the recess to be done in one shallow pass while the corners are squared out with a chisel. You need to make a centre mark that can be lined up with the original centre mark on the door, thus matching the first jig position exactly. The side hole borings can be done in one of two ways. The first method is to add a piece of ¼in (6mm) MDF to the side of the second jig with small holes drilled into it. You can mark the door by pushing a bradawl through these holes and then drill freehand.

Alternatively, you can make holes in the MDF to take a small guide bush and an even smaller cutter with necessary allowances made for the cutter-to-guide-bush diameter, as is usual when doing this type of operation. The small, straight cutter can then produce the rather neat little holes that are required.

It is hard to justify all this effort for just one lock, but the result is satisfying and part of an important learning curve. If you are fitting several locks,

it begins to makes sense, because they can be done very quickly. This is the beauty of jigs and templates – you achieve predictable and reliable results every time.

The intelligent use of templates and jigs can speed up the production of standard parts, also increase the accuracy that is possible, and simplify operations. If you are planning a major project, jigs and templates will make your life easier.

CHAPTER 7

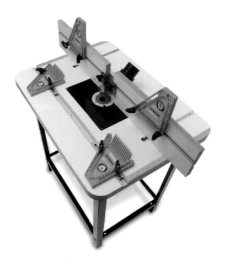

INVERTED ROUTING

You might think of the router primarily as a portable, handheld tool.

Of course, it can be used in this way, although a little experience may

show that this way of working has some shortcomings. Inverted routing,

where the router is set into a table, opens up a whole new way of working.

ROUTING SAFELY WITH CONTROL

Poor visibility, lack of proper control on small or narrow workpieces, inexplicable inaccuracies between supposedly identical components and the inability to undertake difficult operations are just some of the results of working freehand. Freehand is fine, of course, for the right kind of operation, but there are limits. Like a lot of professionals, I use both a ¼in router and a ½in model; the bigger machine spends most of its time upside down under a table. This is because I regard it more as a router spindle, like a small spindle moulder.

The router spindle, with the plethora of cutters now available, from small to extraordinarily large, can now challenge its bigger static cousin, the spindle moulder. It's not quite that simple, of course, but even a small router and a modest table will give neat and controlled results, including stopped operations in which the cut must have a precise beginning and end. Joint cutting is also practical in situations where doing it any other way will produce ill-fitting results. End grain or scribing cuts are also possible.

PROPRIETARY ROUTER TABLES

The shelf-type router table project (pp. 162–165) and the sophisticated router table project (pp. 166–171) offer some ideas for building your own router table. For the moment, we will look at a variety of tables on the market today; these vary from very lightweight plastic to more substantial cast alloy and pressed steel. The old adage that 'you get what you pay for' applies here. If you have purchased a machine such as the Trend T5, which is well-made and has a decent motor rating, don't treat it badly by matching it with a poor table – spend the extra to get a good table that will last and prove its worth.

Many tables are not very large. This is fine for some kinds of work, but long workpieces present a problem. This can be overcome with roller stands if the wood is fairly straight and true. Read up tests in magazines and catalogues and visit stores to look at the goods firsthand. If you are thinking of making a table instead, that is admirable, but bear in mind that a readymade table should have solved all the construction problems. This is a definite plus for the first timer.

The Trend CRT table is compact and rigid. It comes with various essentials such as adjustable fence facings, hold-downs, a mitre protractor and an NVR switch.

A roller stand makes work easier and safer.

■ WHAT TO LOOK FOR IN A ROUTER TABLE

The following are useful features in a router table. Not surprisingly, they don't all come as standard; if they are available, they are often extras that raise the price.

- a large, flat, solid work surface

- a rigid, accurate fence with plenty of space in the opening for large cutters

- proper, effective hold-downs

- a means of fitting extraction

- a safety-type switch (known as an NVR: no volt release) to override the router's own switch

- a mitre fence

- some form of guard over an exposed cutter

- extras such as a roller bearing guide for unfenced work and a lead-in point for safe machining the same work

- some means of securing the table, thereby preventing it from slipping around.

THE TABLE SET-UP

Let's look in detail at each part of the table set-up and some examples. The table itself should be cast aluminium or pressed steel, or a piece of melamine-faced MDF on a metal frame.

Some tables are ribbed to reduce friction on the work and to give the wood dust somewhere to go. Usually, there is a slot running the full length; this is used to hold the mitre fence. This fence allows the ends of components to be machined at 90° (or other angles down to 45° to the fence. To do this, slide the mitre fence forward, pushing the wood towards the cutter and past it until the cut is done. It is possible to use an accurately cut block of wood as a substitute for the mitre fence when doing 90° work.

The table's main fence should be the length of the table with two separate faces and a reasonable-sized gap in the middle where the cutter will be. The fence faces should be capable of accepting wooden facings or one long through-fence that covers the cutter completely. This is good to have when you need maximum work support, especially when machining short ends.

To make a through-fence, switch on the router with the fence in front of the cutter. Then pull the fence back until the cutter breaks through, showing just the right amount of cutting surface to do the intended work.

Both of the basic machined surfaces of the fence should be true to each other; a steel rule placed across both will show just how flat they really are. The centre part for the cutter should give full enclosure to the cutter except the front face. It must have some kind of extraction port to take a hose to a light industrial vacuum cleaner.

Extraction is essential and a cast-off ordinary vacuum may have enough suction, but is unlikely to have sufficient dust-holding capacity. Any machine normally used for domestic cleaning must not be borrowed for this work at all!

Various router tables.

The vital dustspout, which can be linked to a suitable extractor.

A small hole in the sub-fence for cutting skirting gives an unwavering finish, which also applies when cutting short workpieces.

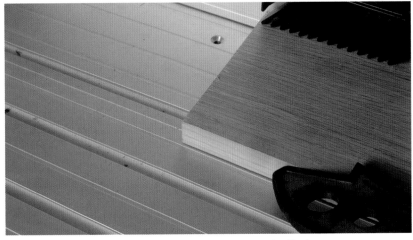

This extractor sits neatly underneath this professional router table.

A ribbed and skeletal table surface allows the workpiece to move unhindered by dust.

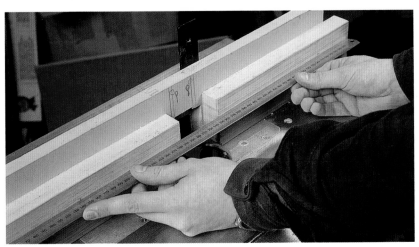

Checking the flatness of a fence (with sub-fences fitted).

★ WORKING TIP

A lot of router table operations can be done in a smallish space, but long workpieces need plenty of infeed and outfeed space and support, especially on the outfeed side. Try and find a place in the workshop where you can do this, possibly utilising a bench surface as the extra support.

HOLDING THE WORK

It is essential that there is some proper way of holding the work while you push it over the table. This will ensure that the the cutter shapes the wood evenly and accurately. You can then concentrate on pushing the work through at an even rate. Work that does not get this kind of pressure tends to be unevenly shaped or moulded, and it will have chatter marks caused by running loose over the cutter. Safety is improved too, because the work is held by the machine and not the operator, except for long lengths that do need additional support. The operator's fingers, which are vulnerable, can be protected by guards that physically obstruct most approaches to the cutter. Generally, there are two sorts of hold-down. One is the now less typical Shaw guard, which consists of a sprung, wood-faced pad pressing onto the workpiece. It can be adjusted to give optimum pressure. Two of them are required for proper support: one vertically, the other horizontally.

The second option is the sprung-finger type, which consists of many diagonal thin tines or fingers pressing against the workpiece. They are fitted so that they lie angled in the direction in which the work is fed and bend a little as the work is forced against them. They can be made from plastic or homemade from MDF. Again, two are required. There are other variations, but they all do the same job and the fence should be fixed firmly enough to resist any pressure exerted by

the hold-downs on the workpiece. Where hold-downs aren't practical, it is better to use a push-stick or push-block.

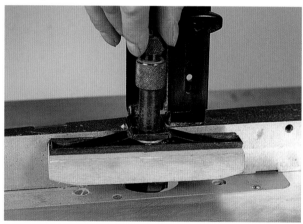

An adjustable sprung Shaw guard.

This operation would be less safe and successful without the use of a push-block.

Holding the workpiece with spring fingers.

EDGE MOULDING

The first, and most common, operation you are likely to do on the table is edge moulding. You take a square or rectangular section of wood and cut a moulding into it. There is little more to it than that, except that the wood must first be square. Softwoods from a timber yard or a do-it-yourself store, when sold in prepared form, are generally square, although a check with a try square or an engineer's square may reveal otherwise. Hardwoods may not be sold in prepared form and may not stay straight and square even if they are sold like that. Access to a planer thicknesser makes all the difference. If the wood is ready to use, it will run tightly to the fence and give a nice even-moulded finish.

Waney-edge board being marked up for cutting. A saw table and a planer are required.

Sawing a moulding from a board. A new moulding can then be made.

Checking the squareness of softwood with an engineer's square.

It is quite possible to mould a small square section, but if you need several pieces it is better to take a wide board, mould the edge, and then cut that moulding off with a circular saw in a table, repeating the process as many times as necessary. This is a more efficient use of the wood and the moulding will be better quality. A small section will vibrate more as it passes over the cutter and with a deep pass may even break up into pieces if the wood has any defects such as short, angled grain or knots.

With a wide board, only the top hold-down can be used, because the table will not be wide enough to fit the other one. Apply side pressure with your hand instead. Many cutters, such as the ovolo and cove, have simple profiles, but there are cutters that cut a complicated shape in one pass.

It is possible to use one or more cutters on the table, and to alter the height or the fence position so that a complicated shape can be built up in several passes.

A lightweight planer, being used in thicknessing mode, reducing stock to an exact size.

A wide board held by hold-down and side hand pressure.

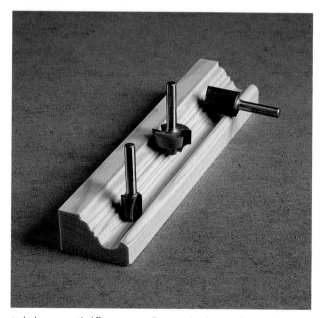

Multiple passes with different cutters allow complex shapes to be created. NB: the straight cut needs to be made from a different position.

BUILDING OUT THE FENCE

A built-out fence can be used for certain moulding operations. You may wish to mould the entire face of a component and, in so doing, make the workpiece narrower. The result is that as you get towards the end of the workpiece it will start to dip in towards the fence and at the very last moment, as it passes over the cutter, the cutter will take a sudden step or chunk out of the workpiece as it drops entirely against the outfeed fence. The answer is to fit a packing piece, of the same thickness as the intended cut, against this part of the fence. You can work out what thickness this needs to be by starting the cut, then stopping the machine and measuring the gap. You can make this packing piece out of thin ply or MDF, or even solid wood, and it can be pinned or screwed into the fence facing. Thus, as the work leaves the cutter it slides smoothly onto the added support. Hold-downs should be used as usual.

Using a spare piece of wood to align the rule when checking how far the cutter projects.

A workpiece with a stepped end.

A workpiece leaving the cutter and about to slide onto a support on the outfeed part of the fence.

DROP-ON MACHINING

This technique requires nerve, as it involves slowly lowering a workpiece directly onto an exposed cutter while also pressing it against the fence. I cannot recommend it as a method for a beginner, but it merits description because it is useful for certain types of work. Using a pocket cutter, one can perform mortising, providing that the fence is marked to show where to start and stop the cut and that the workpiece has datum marks as well. Stop-blocks can also be fitted for this and other stopped operations. They act as a positive means of determining the end of a cut.

Stopped face moulding is also possible. This is where decorative detail is applied to the face of a workpiece, but needs to start and stop short of the ends.

Obviously, good control of the workpiece is necessary to make this kind of operation safe, and this is where the problem arises. If the work is placed on and lifted off by finger grip only, it is quite possible to lose

Dropped-on working. Stop-blocks have been fitted to the fence to determine the length of the mortise.

control. The cutter may grab the workpiece and damage it. The only way to avoid this is to fix some kind of work-holding device onto the workpiece that enables you to grip it and have the full control that is necessary. It follows that most of the time this is not possible, because such devices will mark the surface of the wood with screw- or pin-holes. At no

time should the fingers be exposed to the cutter. Shallow cuts are the only ones that should be attempted by inexperienced routers. This rules out drop-on mortising, but where face-moulding detail is needed and the reverse side isn't seen, it is a good way of adding detail to a piece of furniture.

A damaged dropped-on workpiece. A gentle zigzag downward movement is needed, as well as pressure against the fence. Note how the cutter has blackened because it was plunged too rapidly.

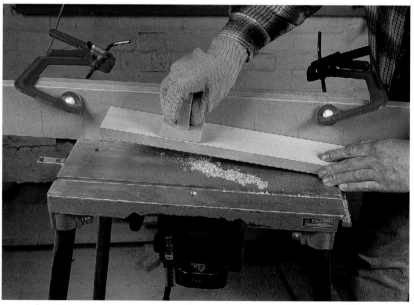

Stopped fluting with the aid of a fixed-on work-holding device. The sticky glove gives the operator a safer grip.

PROFILE-AND-SCRIBE JOINTING

This is a modern jointing idea that has really taken off where cabinet doors are concerned. In the old days, all door frames needed mortise-and-tenon joints to hold them together. The profile-and-scribe has rewritten the rules by using the decorative edge moulding, and the groove behind that holds the door panel, to form one half of the joint. The ends of the top and bottom rails make up the other half, having a matching scribe shape. The joint is tight and interlocking, and will set solid with a little PVA glue.

The term 'scribe', or 'scribing', is regularly used by woodworkers to describe any cut that fits accurately to an existing surface, whether it is a piece of infill wood against a wall in a room or the counterprofile in a joint. Where a joint is concerned, this is invariably done on the end grain or cross grain of the wood and therefore a scribing cut is taken to mean a cross-grain cut. All scribing cuts done on the router table with any type of cutter need proper support behind the wood to prevent breakout.

The scribe part of the joint showing the grain.

An assembled profile-and-scribe joint.

Machining a tenon is a form of scribing cut.

Frame-and-panel door samples: classical, ogee and bevel.

A raised panel and flat panel side by side.

There are about four or five different moulding patterns for profile-and-scribe jointing, including bevel, ogee, classical and ovolo. These are available from a number of suppliers. They normally allow for a door ¾–⅞in (18–22mm) thick with one or two larger sets for doors of 1in (26mm) thickness. These mouldings are ideal for lightweight doors in furniture.

Large joinery-type doors can't be made this way on the router because they are twice the thickness and consequently heavy, although spindle-moulder tooling is available for this size of door.

To complete profile-and-scribe doors, you need either thin, flat-centre panels or a raised solid-wood panel. The latter can be done with a panel-raising cutter, which is available in a number of moulding styles and also in a normal and a vertical type. The vertical type fits easily into a small hole in a router table. These cutters can only be used with 8mm and ½in collets; it is preferable to use the ½in shank sizes because of the stresses involved. The next chapter describes how to use them.

■ BEARING-GUIDED TRIMMING

This subject has already been covered in detail (see p. 92 [Chapter 6]). The router table is ideal for work with bearing-guided cutters.

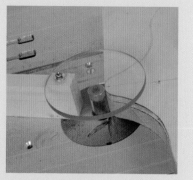

Bearing-guided work on a router table, using a lead-in point.

★ WORKING TIP

Panel raisers are a larger piece of kit and need to be used with respect. They cut a low bevel and a raised edge to the flat centre of the door panel. Some types cut a profile on the reverse that form a tongue to go in the slots of the door frame and is intended to be teamed with a profile-and-scribe door-framing set.

SLOTTING AND REBATING

These are basic requirements and are easily done on the table, and with a better control and finish than is possible freehand. As with all table operations, make sure the work stays flat and slides easily along the fence.

Next, set the cutter the correct distance from the fence. This can be difficult to check properly, because of the hole in the fence opposite the cutter – you can use a Trend gauge to do this accurately. Set the height as well, before machining; this applies whether you are cutting a slot or a rebate – a rebate is just half a slot, after all.

When slotting, the cutter is fully exposed, but once the workpiece is pushed onto the cutter it becomes a temporary guard. Even so, you should be careful about where you put your fingers when pushing the work through. It is important to keep the wood tight against the fence, because it may wander a bit. Smaller cutter sizes can cause the slot to become jammed with tightly packed chippings. In this case it is better to run the wood over the cutter a second time, which should then clear the slot out without any effort. With rebates, you are taking a corner out of the work, so you need to run the work squarely over the cutter without it dipping down. In this case, try using a vertical hold-down or sprung fingers placed over the area that isn't going to be machined.

Test cuts on a spare piece to check cutting width.

A slot and a rebate side by side.

Another method is to make a 'tunnel'. This can be made accurately from ply or MDF. It needs an opening just big enough for the wood to pass through, and the longer it is the better. This tunnel needs to be fixed to the fence in some fashion and, providing the stock you are machining is accurately prepared, it is quick and easy to push it through the tunnel in safety and get a perfectly machined result at the other end. The tunnel method can be used for other moulding shapes as well, unless you are intending to machine away the whole of one face. In this case, the resultant moulding will not have proper support.

Pushing work carefully through with fingers.

Hold-downs and spring fingers for safety and good work control.

A 'tunnel', or an enclosure that is also a hold-down, is the safest method for machining small sections.

■ WORKING METHOD

1 Machine or use stock that is all the same size, as the tunnels do not work properly otherwise.

2 Fit the intended router cutter and position the fence to give the correct cutter projection.

3 Set the correct cutter height and do a test cut of the first section of the workpiece.

4 If the amount to be machined away is quite large, move the fence forward so only a more acceptable amount will be removed on the first pass.

5 Having ascertained the correct setting, you can now make the tunnel. Use offcuts of the workpiece to obtain the correct tunnel shape.

6 If you have a high fence you can clamp a board with a batten fixed underneath, this will press down on the offcuts.

7 You can either pin a side piece to the batten that restricts sideways movement or clamp a board against the side of the offcuts.

8 Remove the offcuts and you are ready to begin machining. Note that if the edge of the stock is being machined away you will need to fix a thin strip on the outfeed fence to give support.

EDGE PLANING

Just as edge planing can be done freehand, so it can be done on the table, only better. Since the fence is quite long, it is just right for straightening edges. A router in a table cannot equal a full-sized planer, and it doesn't give infinitely fine adjustment, but it is still very useful. With the professional spindle moulder, each fence can be adjusted separately; the outfeed fence can be positioned exactly to take off the work as it is planed on the cutterblock. With a router table, we need to do what we did earlier when working

Setting the cutter level with the outfeed fence with the aid of a rule.

Using a straightedge to check for bowing.

freehand: stick strips of the iron-on melamine or the veneer tape to the outfeed half of the fence. These match the depth of the cut; one to three pieces of tape may be needed. The cutter needs to project from the fence by this amount.

If an edge is bowed (that is, convex), you should run the centre part over the cutter before planing the rest of it. This should then true up the edge so that it is acceptably straight and square.

■ BUYING SQUARED TIMBER

It pays to find a decent timber yard selling good-quality softwood and hardwood. They should be able to supply planed and squared hardwood as well as standard softwood ready for use. If the timber happens to be too long to transport, normally the case with softwood, they should be happy to crosscut it to more convenient lengths for you.

I often buy timber this way and it saves a lot of hassle; I do however check it is flat and true first and for any other defects.

CHAPTER 8

MAKING JOINTS

The key to most woodwork is jointmaking. Without joints of some kind it would be impossible to make all sorts of items in wood. Fortunately, the router is very good at making joints, and you won't have to spend money on extra cutters if you don't want to, as in many cases it is possible to use simpler jointing methods. However, with the right cutters you can create very professional-looking cabinetwork and doors if you are prepared to invest in more sophisticated cutters.

JOINTING BASICS

First and foremost, you should prepare the timber properly, because jointing doesn't work well with unsquare and unevenly sized parts. Remember that some matched cutter sets, such as the profile-and-scribe, require one half of the joint to be cut face down, while the other half is cut with the face up. The thickness of the stock is critical and must be the same throughout, or the finished joints will not be flush.

A table saw and an electric planer table are the ideal way to prepare timber, although prepared softwood from a timber merchant is pretty good if chosen carefully. Most measuring and checking can be done with an expanding steel rule, a 12in (30cm) steel rule, and a medium-sized engineer's square – not a carpenter's square, because they are not very accurate. Precise settings on the router table itself can be checked with

vernier callipers. There are some cheap imports and even plastic versions for those with smaller budgets. Since I first wrote this book, technology has moved on and we now have all kinds of digital devices including digital callipers, which are often very cheap to buy. They are really easy to zero and measure with and much easier to read than trying to interpret the scales on traditional ones – highly recommended.

With all cabinetwork, let alone table operations, it is the norm to mark up all chosen faces with a face mark and an edge mark. This means that you have taken the trouble to choose the best face and edge, and it ensures that any operation, such as moulding, is done on the right side, especially when more than one operation is needed. Not surprisingly, some terrible mistakes can occur if this isn't done! A critical factor to check is that the adjacent face and edge that you have chosen are at 90° to each other, which the engineer's square will let you do. The wood needs to be flat in length as well; you can check this by sighting along the wood.

Follow good workshop practice and mark up all components before machining. Also, mark components with their function or size, so that you can sort them into piles for machining, and re-sort them for assembly. Terms such as 'stile', 'rail' and 'muntin', denoting the vertical strips of a door or carcass frame, the top and bottom strips, and the vertical one that sits

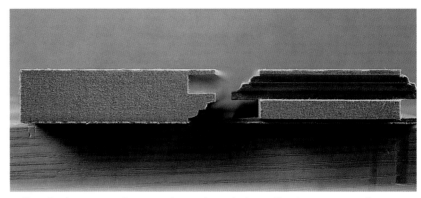

Profile-and-scribe parts in machining attitude to emphasize the face-up/face-down cutting procedure.

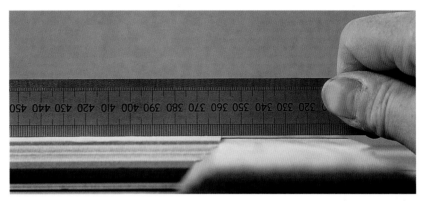

A joint face that is not level.

between the top and bottom rail when a door or panel split into two, respectively, are the usual ways of showing which piece is which. When marking up, abbreviations are handy. Use an H or HB pencil for writing on wood – anything harder will permanently scar the work.

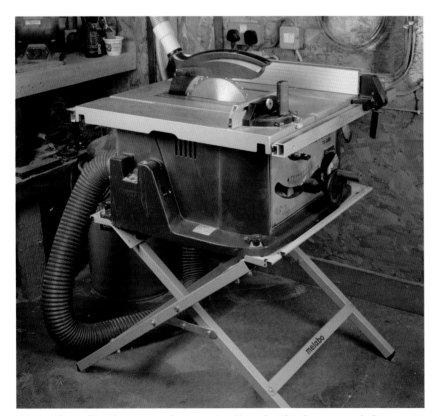

A lightweight portable table saw can produce very acceptable results without having to spend a large amount of money.

★ WORKING TIP

If you are lucky enough to own a saw table then you can size timber how you like. It means that you have much more control over wastage and also the proportions and look of a piece of work. You need a decent quality sharp blade, which should be able to give you a very good cut finish and thus hopefully eliminate a lot of finishing work on sawn edges.

Marking up joints accurately requires a hard, sharp pencil, or better still a small knife or cabinetmaker's awl, because these leave thin lines that are easy to work to. Where machined edges are fluffy, as with the 'fingers' made by a glue joint cutter, or with decorative mouldings, these will all need light sanding before assembly – sanded to a 'finish' in the latter case, because it is almost impossible to do it after it is glued up.

Don't overdo the gluing, especially if there are loose components such as the panel in a frame and panel door. PVA white glue is fine, as is Extramite powdered casein glue, especially for exterior work. There is also carpenter's aliphatic resin that is good and has a high tack rate, meaning that it starts to grip the wood quite quickly. Polyurethane glue is now widely available – this expands before setting, so good clamping is required.

A set of accurate measuring tools is essential for accurate router work.

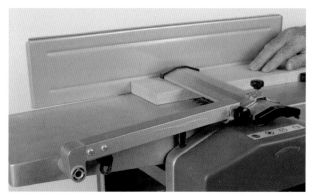

A baby planer thicknesser enables you to take sawn timber and convert it into flat and properly edged sections ready to turn into routed components.

Making a face-and-edge mark.

Correctly stacked components.

An assembled frame with a muntin.

Various tools needed for making joints. From top to bottom: an engineer's square, an awl, a knife and a sharp, hard pencil.

Glues: From left to right: polyurethane, aliphatic resin, PVA, Extramite.

Sash cramps in use.

Fine-sanding mouldings by hand before assembly.

Belt sanding a plain piece of board before moulding the edge. Note the use of a vacuum sanding table thus avoiding cramps getting in the way of the sander.

Use proper cramping methods, such as sash cramps, in order to close the joints, and check that the frames are square and that panels and so on are truly flat once the cramps are tightened. If the glue gets onto the cramps, it can pick up an iron stain, which may be transmitted to the wood. The paper prevents this. When you have cramped everything, wipe off the glue with a damp cloth, or just let the glue go plasticky and scrape it off with a second-best chisel – this avoids raising the grain by getting the wood wet. Once the glue has set overnight, you will need to level the front and back faces of the work, because it is often the case that joints are not as smooth as they should be. Some careful sanding, with a belt sander followed by an orbital sander, for instance, will tidy up the work and give you a good finish.

TONGUE-AND-GROOVE JOINT

The tongue-and-groove is a joint of
long standing and has proved to be
invaluable where large areas need to
be covered with panelling. It is formed
of narrow unglued strips, each of which
has a tongue on one edge and a
matching groove on the other. It may
also have bevelled front edges that form
decorative V-grooves when the joint is
assembled – the whole joint being known
as 'TGV'. An alternative is the loose
tongue; this is glued together to form
a larger rigid panel.

This most basic of joints can be made
with two different kinds of cutter. You can
use a normal straight cutter – a narrow
one – to groove the stock as it passes
through. It should be standing on edge
against the fence. Then you use a wider
cutter, say ¾in (19mm) or bigger, set well
down in the table to cut the tongue.

To do this, lay the workpiece down
and machine from each face in turn
to leave a tongue that will fit the
groove already cut. The results can be
somewhat uneven and the cutter that
does the grooving can come under
strain, especially when the groove
becomes choked with chippings.

A better way to cut these joints is to buy
a dedicated tongue-and-groove cutter
set. This consists of two wide groovers
to cut the tongue, mounted on an arbor
with a bearing to maintain correct

Cutting a groove on the router table with a straight cutter.

depth, and a narrow groover for cutting
the slot. Various manufacturers make
these sets. Generally a router with an
8mm or ½in collet is required.

Make sure that you understand the
order in which the components fit onto
the arbor and the right direction of
rotation. You need to cut the groove
first and the tongue second. A test cut

is necessary and, certainly in the case
of the Wealden set, the groove may
need to be altered by using the shims
(very thin washers) supplied. Mark the
shim, or shims, that give the best fit with
a felt-tip pen so that you can set up
quickly next time. Once you have the
machining set-up worked out, you can
proceed with the actual work.

A tongue-and-groove joint with bead and V-groove for added interest.

Machining the tongue on a small corner block.

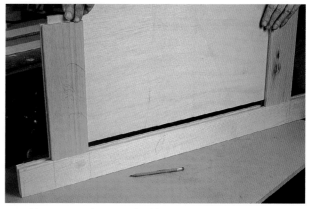

Assembling tongue-and-groove with added panel.

The fence position is also important, so check the instructions to see how deep the groove and how wide the tongue are supposed to be. Usually it will be obvious: these sets generally have a large, mounted bearing, and the diameter of this determines how deep the groovers cut as the work runs against the bearing.

Shaped work can be done without a fence, using a lead-in point instead, but normally you use the straight fence, set so that the bearing is flush with the front.

A straight through-fence facing helps when doing the scribing cuts, because it will allow the end being cut to run smoothly through the cutter without getting unintentionally pushed – this will cause uneven machining on the end. In order to get the cutter to penetrate through the fence, you first need to cut a slot in the facing that will accommodate the arbor and the bearing.

Allow the two groovers to cut their way through the fence as it is drawn back onto the running cutter. Once at the correct position, lock the fence, switch off and check that everything is ready for a test run before machining. Don't jiggle the fence around when pushing it back onto a running cutter – the cutter will catch the fence and kick it away. Make sure there is an off switch close by, too.

Using a straightedge to check that the cutter bearing is flush with the fence.

A large frame-and-panel cutter useful for tongue-and-groove work. The shims allow the fit of the joint to be adjusted.

A damaged scribe cut, caused when the workpiece was pushed into the opening in the fence.

A pre-cut slot in the through fence for the tongue cutter.

Drawing the fence back onto the cutter so the cutter breaks through the wood.

REBATE JOINT

In Chapter 7 we looked at the rebate simply as a rebate in its own right (see p. 109). Here we need to look at it as a joint where two rebates are fitted together as a flush joint or even as a corner joint. If the components are going to be rebated and joined along the long-grain edges, then only a fairly narrow rebate is required, because any kind of joint made with the grain is much stronger than any cross-grain join. This is because the fibres of each piece of wood lie quite sympathetically side by side, pretty much as they did when the timber was part of a living tree. The glue then completes the joint.

Joining end, or cross grain, together or even to the long grain of another piece isn't likely to succeed, because the pores or vessels have been severed through. It is about as effective as trying to rejoin two pieces of garden hose with glue! If we wish to glue two pieces of wood end to end, we need to improve our chances by extending the long-grain surfaces that meet; we call this the half lap joint.

A corner lap joint, and an edge-to-edge lap joint (long grain).

Severed end grain. Note the 'tail' on the trailing edge of the cut.

■ GLUES

Joints usually rely on glue to make them work. Avoid 'craft' glues as these are intended only for light applications. The minimum is a good-quality woodworking PVA (polyvinyl acrylate) glue which is suitable for interior use. There are exterior versions but, even so, weather-exposed joints should be reinforced with nails or screws. Another more advanced glue which is quite widely available is a type that uses aliphatic resin and normally has a slightly yellowish tint. It is 'fast grab' which means it is quick acting and any that gets on already glossy finished surfaces is easy to lift off and it is tough in the joint.

HALF LAP JOINT

By lengthening the rebate, the end-grain surfaces become less important and the joint becomes stronger. However, this is not a suitable method for a joint that will be put under a lot of stress. As with other joints, it is important that your stock is the same thickness.

You are machining only on the 'face side' of both parts and then turning one part over. If they are not the same thickness, you will get a stepped joint. Alternatively, have one piece at 90°, as a flat corner joint for a frame. To machine the half lap joint, you will need to pass over the cutter several times to get the full width of cut. The best plan

An end-to-end lap joint.

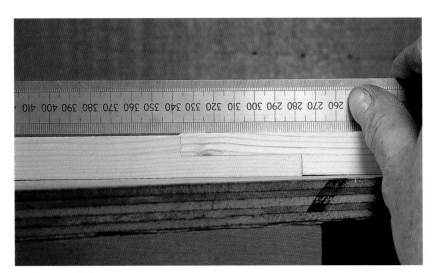

A badly 'stepped' joint.

is to use the straight fence as a length stop for each component and use the mitre fence, as with all scribing cuts, to feed the work over the cutter.

Start at the end and push the workpiece towards the fence by nearly the width of the cutter, before each successive pass, until on the last pass it touches the fence and you have arrived at the full width of cut. Make sure that you have a backing piece of wood screwed to the mitre fence that almost touches the straight fence so that the work is properly supported to minimize breakout.

Cutting a lap on the table – the last pass.

★ **WORKING TIP**

Obtaining level joints is always a potential problem. All stock needs to be the same thickness, of course, but any unevenness in the router table surface or a bow in the timber will prevent flush joint making. Equally, you need consistent downward pressure on workpieces but not directly over where the joint is being machined away.

MORTISE-AND-TENON JOINT

This basic frame joint transfers quite well from the mallet and chisel to the router. I covered it to some extent in Chapter 6 (see p. 96), but whereas the earlier mortises were for locks and hinges, here we look at a complete joint.

Always make the mortise first, because it is easier to make the tenon fit the hole rather than the other way round. This time we are going to make normal frame joints such as you would make for a chair or table underframe. A more appropriate means of controlling the mortising operation is needed, hence a wonderful item called a mortise box. This is a U-shaped trough, accurately made and designed to hold the workpiece in the box while the router slides along the top.

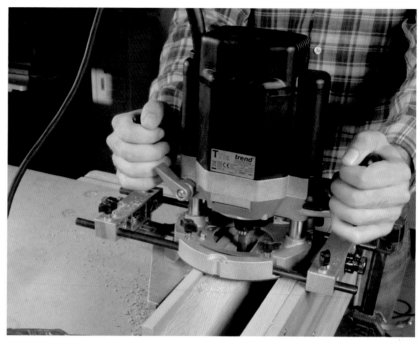

A mortise box. The workpiece is clamped at both ends, while a stop fitted on top limits the length of the socket.

Checking the fit of a typical mortise-and-tenon joint.

Two slim F cramps are needed to hold the workpiece against one side, while the router has to be kept on track by fitting the fence with its rods on one side of the box and a second fence on the other side. Thus, not only will the router run in a straight line, but by undoing its own lock knobs it can be slid across to make passes at different widths to increase the overall width of the mortise. The last thing you need to do is to fit some movable stops at each end so the mortise length can be altered. The depth is controlled by plunging, as usual, and it is vital to put packers under the workpiece to maximize the depth of cut. It is possible that a router without long fence rods or an adjustable fence could be fitted with a thin MDF sub-base instead; this could have strips either side to slide along the sides of the box.

Unless you can buy a special jig for making routed tenons, the easiest way in the workshop is to use the router table and treat tenons as if they were lap joints, except that each tenon is normally 'shouldered' on all four sides instead of just one. This will require four separate operations. Each part will have both faces cut followed by both edges, making a sequence of two operations with different cutter settings for face and edge. Obviously, you need to work out the right proportions for your mortise-and-tenons. This will vary according to the size of wood you are using.

Paring down the tenon corners.

Routed mortises have rounded corners, so you have a choice of either squaring them out with a sharp chisel or rounding off the tenons. Opt for the latter if you are not confident with the chisel. The tenons should be a close fit for the hole, but they should not need to be driven in with a mallet. A little experimentation may be needed to create joints that can be put together without suffering damage; you may need to adjust the cutter height slightly. Another key point is to make the tenons slightly shorter than the hole. This allows room for the glue as the joint closes.

If the mortise box is deep enough, it will even allow awkwardly shaped components to be mortised, so long as the section to be mortised is perpendicular to the cutter.

A close-up of the mortise box holding an angled workpiece. Wedges are used to make it level.

LOCK MITRE OR DRAWER JOINT

This is nothing to do with locks, of course – this rather large and impressive cutter has an interlocking joint shape on the edge, hence the name. The cutter for this comes in two or three sizes and is largely intended for creating 'drawer boxes', or drawers to you and me. The box is the basis for modern drawers, having a front panel put on it afterwards to finish it off, whereas on traditional drawers the front is integral to the drawer.

Cutting the vertical part of a drawer lock joint.

A drawer box taken apart to show the groove for the bottom panel. When installed, the front will oversail the sides to hide the drawer runners.

The lock mitre is used on all four vertical corners and needs sequenced machining. One half of each joint is cut with the component lying down on the table, while the other half is cut with it standing up against the fence. Note that a high fence facing has been fitted for precise, safe support. Certain other operations, such as panel raising, also require a high fence, otherwise the cut can be uneven and the operation can be precarious. Test cuts are vital to achieve good results, so keep some spare pieces of wood handy for this purpose.

In addition to the mitres, the drawer bottoms need to be fitted. The slots for these can be made with a straight cutter or a groover before assembling the box. Cramping is critical – if the pressure is applied too far from the corners, the mitres can 'yawn', or open up, and the drawer sides will be bowed.

A drawer box that has been badly cramped, causing the joint to open.

BISCUIT JOINTING

My favourite joint method by far is the biscuit plate or spline. I use a jointing machine most days, but on the grounds of cost and for certain difficult jointing situations the router has the advantage. There are various cutter sets on the market, including economy and professional-quality sets. Each consists of a groover large enough to cut the slot needed and three bearings so that slots for each of the three standard biscuit sizes can be made. The economy type varies from

A typical professional biscuit jointer. The blade slot is at the bottom in the blade housing.

The CMT three-wing and the Trend Craft Range two-wing biscuit cutter sets, with the three standard biscuit sizes and the Lamello red-barbed assembly biscuit.

the professional one in having a two-bladed cutter instead of a three- or four-bladed one. For occasional use that will be fine – the heavier-duty version is only really necessary for regular use.

Each 4mm-thick, elliptically shaped biscuit is cut from compressed beech with the grain running diagonally to prevent it breaking when the joint is together. There are three standard sizes: 0, 10 and 20. These cope with all the usual-sized joints. There are various specialized types as well, although these are really only of interest to professional users, especially as they are expensive.

BISCUIT JOINTING WITH A ROUTER

The router method is slightly different to the biscuit jointer. The first factor is that the machine needs to be plunged so that the cutter is approximately in the middle of the board to be slotted. Once plunged, it must stay like this until the machine has been moved away from the workpiece. Unplunging while in the wood will cause the slot to be widened, making it useless. The other factor is that biscuits are meant for use with a jointer machine that has a blade 3¹⁵⁄₁₆in (100mm) in diameter, whereas a groover is much smaller. Because the slot is shorter, it is necessary to make a second mark each time and slide the router up to it to elongate the slot. The radius at each end of the slot does not conform to the biscuit shape, but it still works reasonably well. One last point is that the router can only cut butt, edge-to-edge joints or corner joints. This covers most things, but the jointing machine can work T-joints well away from any edge. You can make mid-panel joints with a router and a 4mm straight cutter, but the slot is square-ended and less effective for jointing, especially as the corners will fill up with glue that may not set quickly.

The joints marked up and the slots cut; biscuits standing by.

Butt and corner joints. The T-joint is only possible using a ⅛in (4mm) straight bit or a jointer machine.

To make a biscuit joint, first make two marks across both components, spaced apart to the slotter diameter and bearing size being used. Do this at every point where a biscuit joint is required – usual spacing is 6–10in (150–250mm). Set up your router and cutter, set at the mid-point of the board thickness. Switch on and push sideways into the wood opposite the first mark and move up to the second mark to elongate the slot (cutter advancing in the correct direction). Run a small amount of PVA glue into each slot and insert a biscuit. Close the joint with cramps. After a while the biscuits, having been compressed in manufacture, begin to swell up and grip the sides of the slot, helped by a hatched-grip pattern on each side.

Once the glue has dried, a neat, invisible and strong joint is formed. It is an ideal joint for carcass construction (see room skirting and architrave project, pp. 218–223, and bedside cabinet project, pp. 184–193) because of the low cost and ease of use, many biscuits can go into a piece of furniture, often substituting for conventional methods.

What is hard to describe on paper is just how fast and easy it really is. I would recommend it to anyone, even a relative beginner.

A 'tunnel', or an enclosure that is also a hold-down, is the safest method for machining small sections.

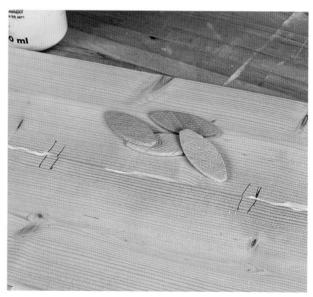

The joint glued together. Note the two marks needed for each slot.

• Apart from normal carcass material such as chipboard, ply and MDF, the biscuit can be used on solid wood. Large sections can be effectively joined using two rows of biscuits for extra strength. The machining should only be done from one face to avoid misalignment between the rows of slots, because the resultant joint will not then close.

• Biscuits are a perfect locational aid and can be used to ensure that corners of carcasses come together square even if some screws are also used to tighten the whole thing up. Kitchen cupboards and wardrobes are good examples of this 'locate and fix' method. It also works when gluing and cramping large surfaces together. Boards can slip out of alignment when being cramped, because glue tends to be slippy – a few biscuits will ensure this doesn't happen.

• A pencil can damage a surface finish such as veneer or lacquer, so run masking tape along both sides of the joint and mark this instead. The router can sit on the tape while it slots and the tape can be peeled away later.

• Place the biscuits 6–10in (150–250mm) apart for adequate strength. There are exceptions to this; narrow components can take biscuits very close together if necessary, becoming in effect a semi-continuous tongue and groove.

• Always use the biggest biscuit practicable. I use No. 20 most of the time. You can buy boxes of 1,000 biscuits containing an assortment of all three sizes, which saves buying too many of one particular size. Keep your biscuits in polythene bags or boxes to prevent them from getting damp, as this will make them swell up.

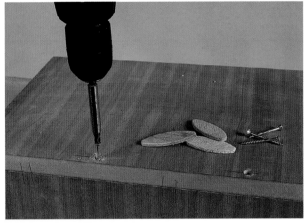

The biscuits help to locate each part of the carcass while the screws fix them together.

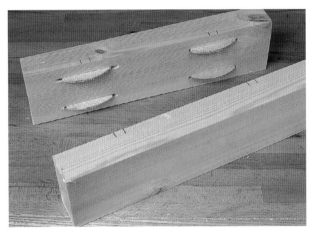

A double row of biscuits in large-section timber.

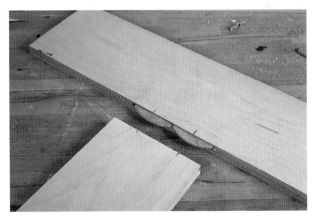

Biscuits used to make a tongue.

CHAPTER 9

DOVETAILING

Dovetail jointing is synonymous with cabinetmaking, just as the mortise-and-tenon is with joinery. Years ago, proper handmade dovetailed drawers predominated. Times have changed, and although some skilled craftspeople still cut dovetails by hand, machine-based methods have largely taken over.

MACHINE-MADE vs HANDMADE

The dovetail combines skill, visual appeal and incredible strength, because the shape of the very aptly named 'tails' interlock with the opposing 'pins'. The dovetail comes in a variety of types, some purely functional, others much more decorative. For years now, there have been fairly simple jigs available for routing dovetails. These have been joined more recently by a handful of much more sophisticated jigs,

designed not only to copy some of the finer examples of hand dovetailing, but also to push back the technical boundaries and thus produce new varieties of joint that have not been possible before. I have cut dovetails by hand in the past, but I would describe my ability as average. I have tried out simple dovetail jigs, to see if they deserved a place in my workshop, but the resulting joints looked rather 'machine-

made'. However, there is some merit to using them, because they add strength to any construction. The more sophisticated jigs are very expensive, but also very good, and create precise and exotic jointwork. Weigh up both your level of skill with the router, and with woodworking generally, and decide whether you really need one of these jigs when there are alternative jointing methods available.

A typical dovetail joint, largely unseen when used on drawers.

A finished joint produced on the Trend jig.

USING A JIG

This is a brief description of how to use the DeWalt/Festool/Bosch-type jig. These jigs are formed of pressed steel and can be cramped or screwed to a workbench. There are two clamping bars: one on top and one on the front. These hold the two components that form the two halves of the joint. On the top, there is also a piece of plated steel with U-shaped cutouts on which the router sits.

To use the jig, the correct dovetail cutter must be fitted. All dovetail jigs require a specific cutter, or cutters, and guide bush for correct use; most manufacturers' cutter ranges have these cutters noted in the specification, so it is easy both to identify and to buy them from different sources. The cutter is set at a specific depth, generally using a little setting-up device. In addition, fitting a fine-depth adjuster to the router helps you to achieve precise depth setting and prevents the router from suddenly unplunging and damaging the jig or cutter.

Once you have preset the depth of cut, you must clamp the boards to the jig. The vertical position cuts the tails, which are all separated from each other, the horizontal clamping position holds the piece, which will have the 'sockets'

machined into it (these are joined continuously). The router runs along on top of the shaped template, going in and out of each U-shape, thus creating each joint shape. It is necessary to try out some test pieces to get the correct fit before cutting into vital components. Typical uses for these 'common dovetails', as they are known on account of their even spacing, would be for small carcasses with exposed jointwork or for drawer boxes. These jigs can also be converted for making square finger joints, which I feel are better-looking, although not so rigid and self-locking as the dovetail. The Bosch and certain other jigs can also be used to make dowelled joints.

LIGHTWEIGHT JIGS

There are several jigs on the market consisting of not much more than a hard plastic or alloy jig that is then screwed to a strip of wood for use, or that can be used to create longer copies of the original jig for wide boards. These have some merit and are worth investigation. The Gifkins jig is one such example. All these jigs need the right cutters; these are usually specified or supplied by the jig manufacturer.

The Gifkins jig – a simple dovetailing solution. Lower cost is also an appealing feature.

★ WORKING TIP

When you machine dovetails it is easy to unintentionally make both pins and tails slightly short so they sit below the surface of the component they fit into. This doesn't look good but it can be allowed for. When you do a test joint, make both halves slightly longer than required by no more than a millimetre or so. Chances are when the joints are assembled they will still project slightly but it doesn't matter as it is fairly easy to plane and sand them flush.

CLEVER JIGS

'Clever' jigs such as the Leigh, Incra and Woodrat are simple in theory but more complicated in practice, partly because of the profusion of scales and adjustments. They are made to very fine engineering tolerances and need to be looked after properly. They are ideal for anyone who likes a challenge and aspires to excellence.

The Incra LS Standard Fence System

An all-American device, this is an impressive affair with precision-milled knobs and various add-on scales. The Incra jig allows you to make cuts in precise and repetitious positions so you can accurately produce dovetails and finger joints of all types and sizes. It is not intended for heavy-grade work, but for fine cabinet joints and boxes. One of these is the double-double box joint – an Incra-created 'joint within a joint'. There are plenty of other possibilities. A lower-cost 'Ultra-Lite' version is also available, with most of the features offered by its big brother.

The LS Standard has a clamp-and-lock system backed up by add-on scales. It looks confusing (and is) and requires a methodical mind to get the right result from it. The jig is fixed to a piece of board that is itself clamped to the router table. Once correctly aligned to the cutter in use, the jig then gives precise data from which each cut can be set up accurately. The fence part has a sliding

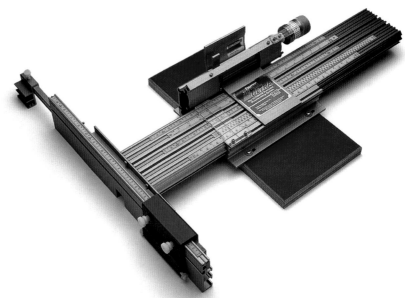

Incra LS Standard jig. A clever gadget that needs plenty of practice to master properly.

end-stop for doing stopped work and there is a push-block also made from extrusions. It is possible to use this jig as a super-accurate saw-table fence, although this would depend on the quality of the table and blade, and would make the Incra jig vunerable to damage by the blade.

A Master Reference Guide and Template Library are available from Incra, showing life-size joints and the matching scales that are needed for making them. This is a very focused fine-jointing system for the dedicated dovetail enthusiast, but possibly not the right gadget for the rest of us.

The Leigh Dovetail Jig

The original Leigh jig is not dissimilar to the DeWalt/Festool jig, but is much more versatile and very precise. This model has now been superseded by the DR4 Pro Dovetail Jig (see bottom left); there is also the R9 Plus Joinery System, which bears some similarities to the Gifkins model.

The operating basics of the new version are similar to the original Leigh jig. The components are clamped on top and in front, while a bar over the top carries a series of shaped alloy fingers. These slide along and can be locked wherever they are needed; a sliding scale allows front-to-back adjustment.

The latest model of Leigh jig.

The adjustable jig bars are set for a 'common' dovetail.

Machining the sockets or pins ready to accept the tails.

The router sits on the fingers and is moved in and out between the fingers in order to form the two halves of the joint. What makes the Leigh special is the build quality and its adjustability, coupled with its own range of HSS cutters and, most importantly, a complete range of guide bushes and mounting plates for all known routers. These guide bushes are vital for the Leigh jig to operate properly. There is also an adjustable mortise-and-tenon jig and a precision-machined finger-joint jig with a variety of joint sizes available. With its comprehensive user guide, and its ability to make shelf stud holes and dovetail housings, this is a versatile and efficient system for any really keen woodworker.

The Woodrat WR900

This ingenious British-made router jig is well thought out and versatile. The Woodrat can cope with a range of components, from the very small to quite large joinery items. It works best in wall-mounted mode, which, if you have a spare piece of workshop wall, makes for a very compact means of working.

The jig consists of a strong, precision-made piece of aluminium box extrusion. There is a plate on top, to which the router is attached, and there are two clamping positions on the front for the workpiece. The router is wound by a handle from side to side, allowing it to be moved carefully to each machining position. It is then pulled forward to make each cut of the joint. The router can be swung from side to side within preset limits, so that dovetail pins can be cut as well as the tails, although the two operations need different cutters. Being very sharp and efficient, Woodrat's own HSS cutters work much better than tungsten-carbide cutters on natural timbers, provided they are kept razor-sharp with frequent honing; when they are blunt you can hone them quite easily. One clamping position is used to hold the component that has the tails marked on it, while the other position holds the one that

is being cut using the first set of markings as a guide. They are then swapped over to complete the joint.

This device can also cut lap, tongue, finger, mortise-and-tenon joints, housings, and even profile joints, making it far more than just a plain dovetail jig. An interesting feature is its ability to safely backfeed.

The Babyrat WR600 model is also available. It is, in effect, half a Woodrat with limitations on capacity and features. It is useful if your budget doesn't stretch to the larger model.

The Trend DC400

This is a heavy-duty dovetail jig, which is decidedly weighty to move around. It has a set of adjustable carbon-fibre fingers, not unlike the Leigh jig. They can be interchanged for two other types, enabling the production of a variety of tails with different angles and lapped pins. A key feature is accuracy and repeatability by clicking the guide fingers into the index strip; this enables spacing increments of $\frac{1}{8}$in (2.5mm). It is not cheap, but it is good.

The Woodrat can perform some impressive tricks.

Trend DC400. One of several Trend dovetail jigs, this recent creation is very heavily built and capable of variable pitch settings similar to the Leigh.

DOVETAIL HOUSINGS

Unlike the dovetail joint, the dovetail housing does not require one of the jigs described on page 129. The difference is that the housing is one long sliding dovetail on the end of a board, which then fits into a matching slot on a carcass. It is a neat, strong, invisible joint and it can be made with a homemade jig. The dovetail also resists movement across the width of the board – the board cannot bow or warp out of shape, because it is locked in place. As it isn't glued, both boards are free to shrink or expand across the grain without splitting.

The housings can be run over a dovetail cutter in the router table. Use a protractor fence to push them and have a stop-board clamped across the table to limit the cut if this is required (i.e. a stopped housing). You will need a jig for larger pieces so that the router can sit on the work to rout the slots. This can take the form of a T-square jig, which has a slot down the middle to take a guide bush. Across the end there is a bar to locate it against the edge of the component. Fix it in position with a couple of cramps. If the slot is long, you can put scale marks along the side so that you can machine housings of different lengths.

It can be difficult to get the right fit with dovetail housings. Sometimes just running the workpiece over a dovetail cutter a second time and pressing more tightly at the same time can be enough to ease the fit.

The other part of the joint, the tail, is done vertically on the table, with the cutter just protruding far enough out of the fence. It is important to have nice flat components and to press them firmly against a high fence for good support. Efficient sideways hold-downs will help too. All this is necessary because it is easy to create a poor joint. Various test cuts are required to get the fit as snug as possible. It should be possible to tap the joint together with a mallet and block, but without using excessive force. Long boards can be cut freehand overhead, using an L-jig.

With stopped joints, the tails need to be cut at one end. This can be done after you have cut the sides of the joint – you will need a protractor fence with a high facing. Breakout around the end of the joint can occur, although it will almost certainly be hidden once the joint is closed. The end of a stopped tail also has to be rounded in order to fit the slot. A little judicious chisel work is called for and will remove any torn corners. With this joint it is possible to assemble a whole carcass, such as a bookcase or shelf, quite successfully; it will be very rigid even without a back panel.

A slotted T-square for cutting housings with a guide bush.

Cutting a dovetail for a housing on the router table.

Cutting the end of a dovetail to fit a stopped housing. Note the high facing fitted to the mitre fence.

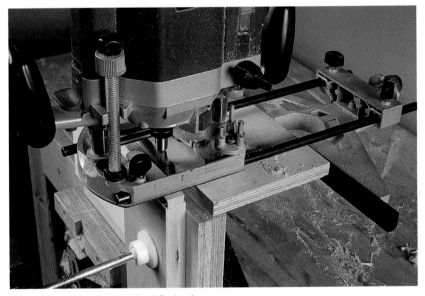

Cutting a dovetail on a long board end (freehand), using an L-jig.

CHAPTER 10

ROUTER ACCESSORIES

There are a huge number of accessories and gadgets available that are either specifically designed for use with the router or that work well with it.

Here we review a selection of these clever gadgets that might interest the reader.

WORKING OUT WHAT YOU NEED

Some of these gadgets are expensive or are not suitable with lightweight machines, but are worth bearing in mind for the future. You can keep yourself up-to-date with new products by looking at woodworking magazines and websites.

Quite a few of these accessories come from the USA, but are also available in the UK, where Trend, in particular, offers every conceivable piece of router-related kit with many accessories.

They use the Trend Base Configuration (TBC), a standardization of the alignment for guide-bush holes, fence holes and table fixings so any machine with that configuration will accept TBC accessories. Other manufacturers' accessories with the same configuration can simply be interchanged. This makes it much easier to use what you want on any router, thus expanding its ability and increasing accuracy. Axminster Tools also supply a variety of router-based accessories. Don't

feel that you need to rush out and buy these accessories – most people don't. However, if you have the need and the money, the solutions are certainly out there.

In this chapter we look at the main manufacturers and survey some of the most useful products that they currently offer. We also look specifically at a number of devices concerned with height adjustment, as this facility is vital in router use.

KREG

Kreg make a number of high-quality router table products, including tables large and small, tabletop insert plates and mitre fences. Kreg first made their name by creating the Kreg Pocket Hole Jig for joining carcasses together.

KREG PRECISION MITRE FENCE

This sophisticated mitre fence features positive stop positions for standard settings and a vernier scale allowing adjustments to 0.1 of a degree. It also features a length stop so that you can machine components with repeatable accuracy.

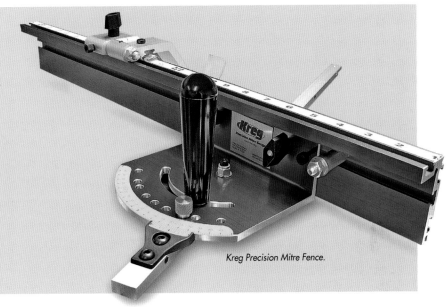

Kreg Precision Mitre Fence.

VERITAS

Veritas have an established reputation for innovative engineering applied to all sorts of woodworking tools, principally hand planes, marking tools and router accessories. Quality comes at a price, but it is worth the investment if you are serious about routing.

VERITAS PIN GUIDE

Veritas have a whole table system, but one unusual item is the Pin Guide. This replicates the ability of a big industrial pin-guided router, in that the pin above the cutter can follow a template pinned to the workpiece while the otherwise unguided cutter underneath simply does the cutting. This makes difficult-shaped work possible without resorting to a bearing-guided cutter. It only works with the relatively thin rolled-steel Veritas tabletop.

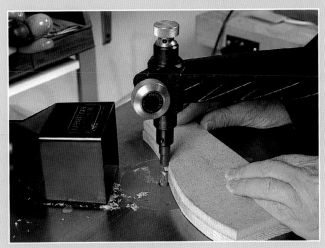

Veritas Pin Guide.

HEIGHT ADJUSTMENT

Router users often become obsessive about improving the accuracy of their work, with good reason. If you want a precise result you need the means to achieve it. The first area of concern is height adjustment.

Simple fine-height adjusters are available: there are various models that simply allow you to wind the router up and down. However, this has limitations, not least the slow speed of adjustment, which necessitates removing the adjusters for 'ordinary' work where the convenience of quick plunging is more useful.

A number of more sophisticated types offer different advantages and are often intended for table use where safe, accurate and easy height changing is crucial. Unless you have only an entry-level router that cannot accept a fine adjuster, I would recommend that you buy some sort of fine adjustment; it is bound to be useful, especially for table work or fine work. In this case it is critical that the cutter cannot be allowed to unplunge and damage itself or the guide bush and the jig!

ROUTERRAIZER

This US-built device fits many different models. It looks, and is, simple in use, despite appearing complicated when you take it out of the box. If you work through the instructions carefully it doesn't take long to fit, although removing the router body from the plunge columns can be unnerving to the beginner. When the Routerraizer is installed, it allows you to alter the plunge settings, use the turret depth-stop and, crucially, allows very fine adjustment via the knob on top or through the base when inverted in the table. The speed wrench makes this adjustment quick and precise.

Routerraizer (US): the speed wrench is removed when the height is set.

WOODRAT PLUNGEBARS

The plungebar is a simple concept that is unique to Woodrat. It has appeared in several versions; this is the easiest and most simple to remove when not required. It is effective both for table and freehand use. It fits a standard TBC or 'clone' model base as well as being available to suit other models. It doesn't involve any alterations apart from removing the fence, thereby precluding fence work. However, you can clamp on a straightedge or use a guide bush. To operate, simply squeeze the bars to plunge the machine. Although it doesn't give fine adjustment, it does allow quick plunging to depth, especially under a table.

A DeWalt router fitted with plungebars; these do not inhibit use in freehand mode although intended for table work.

ROUTER ELEVATOR

The Router Elevator is intended to be fitted into a machined recess in a wooden router table top (melamine-faced is favourite for 'slip'). It is a heavy, well-engineered unit that may seem a bit excessive. However, once in place it holds any router securely. The router can be accessed for cutter changing just by pushing up the Router Elevator. The crucial element is the detachable drive handle that raises the router up and down. It is quick, reliable and very precise.

Router Elevator.

MICROFENCE

The Microfence has been around for some time, although I have yet to meet any router users who own one. This is a pity because it makes fine fence adjustment truly easy compared to the manufacturers' own poor offerings which rarely perform well. For those of us who value the need for accurate and easy fence settings, it is worth the investment.

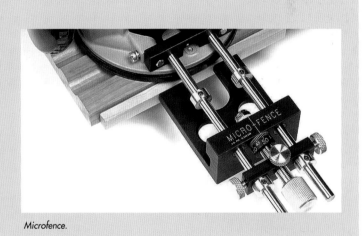

Microfence.

ACCURATE FENCE

A newer introduction from the USA, this not only makes for easy fence setting, its main role is to allow quick, accurate, repeat housings including dovetailed ones. An accompanying Quicktime movie CD shows how this is achieved. Briefly, a scrap of the shelf material to be housed is clamped between the components of the Accurate fence after the first cut made against a T-square, ready for the second pass. Miraculously, the cutter is therefore offset just enough to give the correct fit. If it is tight, a slip of paper is added to ease the fit. The beauty of this fence is the ease of repetition cutting which you need when working on a carcass with a lot of shelves.

Accurate fence.

TREND LTD UK

Trend have long been devoted to producing cutters for routers, but now have an extensive catalogue of routers and accessories. There is only room for a few items here. Their catalogue features a vast range of standard and specialist cutters for trade and DIY users. They also manufacture a series of routers and various jigs or different routing operations.

ELLIPSE JIG

It is possible to make your own jig for creating different-size ellipses, but Trend make it easy with this nifty gadget – no tricky calculations required! It is well worth considering if you are keen to create frames or tablets in this shape.

Ellipse jig.

MORTISE-AND-TENON JIG

Repetitive mortise-and-tenon cutting becomes a doddle with this. Rounds or square-ended tenons are possible, and angle components can be clamped against the jig. Double mortise-and-tenons, and loose tenons, can be made as well.

Mortise-and-tenon jig.

ROUTABOUT

This is a handy device for the professional when creating under-floor access points. Once cut, a plastic ring is inserted so the cutout circle can be put back as a lid for future access. Good for electrics and plumbing.

Routabout.

PIVOT FRAME JIG

This jig allows ski operations for cleaning up groundwork. It works as a beam trammel and can create scallop and decorative patterns. It does this by the user making a round base which the jig can then be clamped around, so the rollers can run easily but accurately around the edge without any free play.

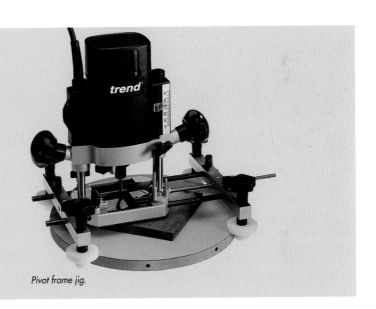

Pivot frame jig.

NUMBER AND LETTER TEMPLATES

These take away the hard work of creating neat shapes quickly, and are useful for making items such as nameboards. As with all plastic jigs used with guide bush and cutters, care is needed to avoid damaging the template in use.

Number and letter templates.

ROUSSEAU

Another US company, Rousseau, make a variety of router tables and machine supports. They also make quite a few specific router accessories, these include fences and a table insert plate with reducing rings.

FREEHAND GUARD

This accessory can be installed in a router table insert plate. It allows safe working using a bearing guided cutter in the router table. The post is used as a lead-in pin, before the workpiece runs onto the cutter with the earings.

JIGGE TRACK

This mitre gauge track gives a precise running fit for a mitre gauge and various other Rousseau accessories including those surveyed below.

FEATHERBOARD

Made from a tough-grade plastic, it flexes but gives firm workholding pressure. Two or more can be used on a table.

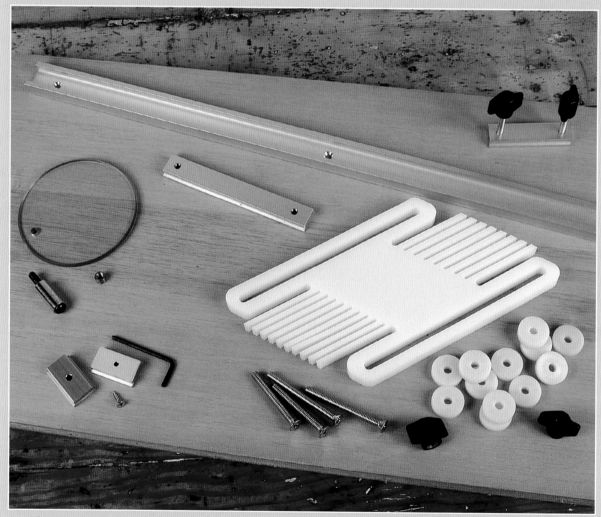

From left to right: Freehand guard, jigge track and featherboard. The other components shown are used in track support.

INCRA

Incra are an American company that first came to the woodworking world's attention with the original Incrajig. Since then they have developed ever-more sophisticated fence systems based on aluminium extrusions, which allow precise machining and joint cutting.

INCRA WONDERFENCE

The smart Wonderfence for router tables replaces the original Intellifence. It is not cheap but it is very precisely made and has various features that put it far above the competition. It features a number of adjustments, built-in extraction and a high work support for vertical working. It is compatible with Incra's saw fences. This is not for the careless user who might regret accidentally damaging this precision piece of kit.

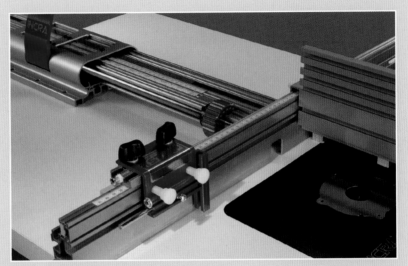

Incra Wonderfence.

THE LEGACY

THE LEGACY

As with so many router gadgets, the Legacy comes from the USA. It is available in two sizes although the longer 48in-capacity version is more popular. It is very sophisticated and has a price to match. With a router installed it becomes a complete workcentre, capable of amazing results once its abilities are understood by the user. It can flatten stock, create tapers, do turnery, spirals, XYZ axis milling, and make housings and mortises. It has indexing for precise alignment of spirals, slots and so on, and it can be hand- or motor-driven. Extra-length cutters are available to give the right degree of reach into the workpiece.

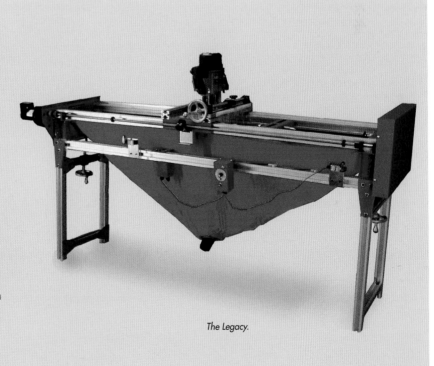

The Legacy.

PROJECTS
FOR THE WORKSHOP

T-SQUARE CUTTING JIG

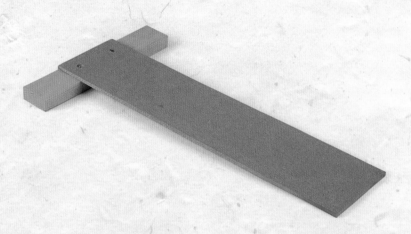

One of the most basic bits of kit after the standard fence must be

a means of machining slots or trimming boards across the grain.

Your best bet is to make your own: it is quick, easy and gives a reliable

means of speedily and accurately machining your work.

● MATERIALS AND TOOLS

- Length of 9mm or 12mm MDF approx. 4in (100mm) wide x suitable length for intended work; 27½in (700mm) long if workpiece is likely to be 23⅝in (600mm) wide

- Short length of 2 x 1in (50 x 25mm) PAR (prepared all round) batten

- PVA glue

- Several 1in (25mm) panel pins

- Hammer

- Try square

1 Cut a strip of 9mm or 12mm MDF for the long arm of the T-square. Cut a shortish piece of prepared softwood batten and pin and glue the MDF to the batten.

2 Check the batten is exactly at 90° to the MDF before the glue has a chance to set. You may be able to tap it gently to correct it. Leave the T-square to dry after wiping away any surplus glue.

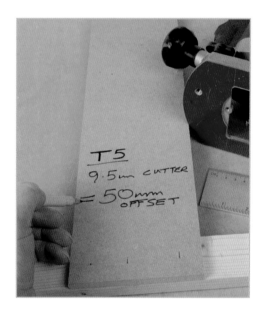

3 It is best to use just one size of straight cutter; mark the offset distance between the cutter and the edge of the router base on the T-square. This means each time you use it you know how much to offset the T-square so the cutter machines to the intended line.

4 A typical use is for machining the dogleg joint in kitchen worktops. Make sure the T-square is always firmly clamped in position. It can also be used with a circular saw for making 90° cuts.

■ USES OF THE T-SQUARE

The T-square, if it is accurately made, is an invaluable device around the workshop that goes beyond routing. Apart from the edge-trimming example shown opposite in step 4, you can use it for making mid-panel biscuit-joint slots using a 4mm-diameter straight cutter. It can be used for marking out just like a technical-drawing T-square and it can be used with a circular saw for crosscutting boards. Note however, that a circular saw will trim off one end of the T the first time it is used like that, in which case make sure the other end of the T is longer to compensate. Another use is checking how square a cabinet carcass really is or if the sides are bowing under clamping pressure. So, a quite simple device is actually very versatile and you may want more than one in different lengths. A last touch is to drill a hanging hole so it is handy but out of the way.

★ WORKING TIP

You can also use the T-square to help with technical drawings. If you use an ink pen, apply some iron-on tape underneath it to prevent the ink running.

The finished T-square cutting jig.

HOUSING JIG

A development of the T-square is the housing jig. In this version,

a guide bush runs in a slot so the router cannot deviate off course.

This makes it more precise for machining carcass housing joints.

● **MATERIALS AND TOOLS**

- Length of 9mm or 12mm MDF approx. 4¾in (120mm) wide x suitable length for intended work; 27½in (700mm) long if workpiece is likely to be 23⅝in (600mm) wide

- Short length of 2 x 1in (50 x 25mm) PAR (prepared all round) batten

- PVA glue

- Several 1in (25mm) panel pins

- Hammer

- Try square

- 16mm guide bush

- 16mm straight cutter

- 9.5mm straight cutter

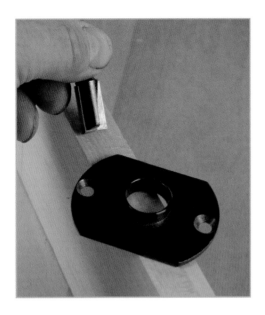

1 First choose a suitable cutter and guide bush combination. Here, a 9.5mm straight cutter is teamed with a 16mm-diameter guide bush.

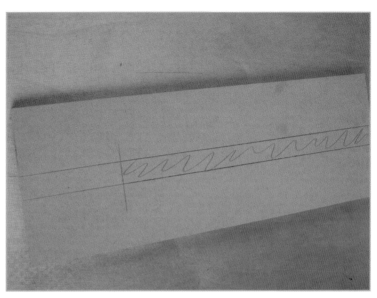

2 Draw out the 16mm slot needed for the guide bush to run in and a limited mark at the end that will have the batten.

3 Cut a slot with a 16mm straight cutter and guide fence, taking care to stay on track so you achieve an accurate slot (leave the MDF overlength so the router has a long running surface). If you have a decent table saw, you can do this operation on there too. Check that the fit is good.

4 Now glue and screw the batten fence in place, checking that it is square and that the slot remains parallel from end to end. Wipe off any surplus glue and leave to set.

■ USES OF THE HOUSING JIG

Whereas the T-square is suitable for edge trimming, the housing jig is the right sort of guidance if you don't want the router veering off course at all. It also gives better support to the base as it prevents the router from tilting. Unlike the T-square it is only to be used with a guide bush, which must be the same diameter as the width of the slot in the jig or the router will deviate as you machine with it.

Dovetail housings are the obvious use for this jig but of course you can make plain housings for shelves to tenon into. Another use is to create stopped slots which can be 'blind' or through slots such as you might want if you have through tenons in a bench leg. To do this you need to screw stops onto the jig to limit router movement along the slot.

You do not need to use the same diameter cutter either. If you want to fit thin divider panels in a carcass, swap over to a 6.4mm cutter that will make slots for 6mm ply or MDF.

Suppose you want to inlay a veneered surface. The housing jig will keep a straight slot and you simply fit the right cutter set to give a very shallow slot. The housing jig is obviously more versatile than you could imagine.

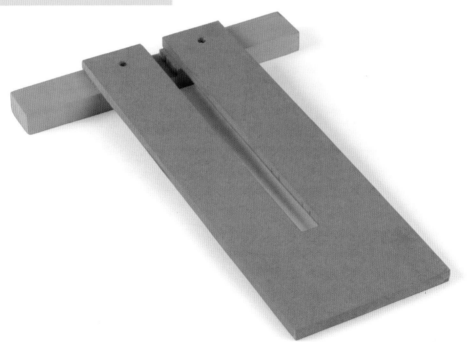

The finished housing jig.

CUTTER SELECTION BOARDS

Storing cutters in a way that keeps them ready for use is often a bit of a nuisance.

They can be in cases or in single packets or worse still, simply loose clanking against each

other. I wanted to find a better, more accessible way of storing them especially as I have

rather a lot of cutters. This design of storage means they are easy to see and to access.

Each board can be lifted off the wall as required; the inverted U-shape underneath

makes it easy to pick them up again. The boards simply drop

onto matching L-shapes fixed to the wall.

● **MATERIALS AND TOOLS**

- Board offcuts of 18mm
  MDF approx. 17 x 5⅛in
  (430 x 130mm)

- Board offcuts of 9mm MDF
  in strips

- Offcuts of prepared softwood
  batten

- 1½in (40mm) twinfast screws

- PVA glue

- Medium abrasive paper
  and disc

- 6.4mm and 12.7mm straight
  cutters

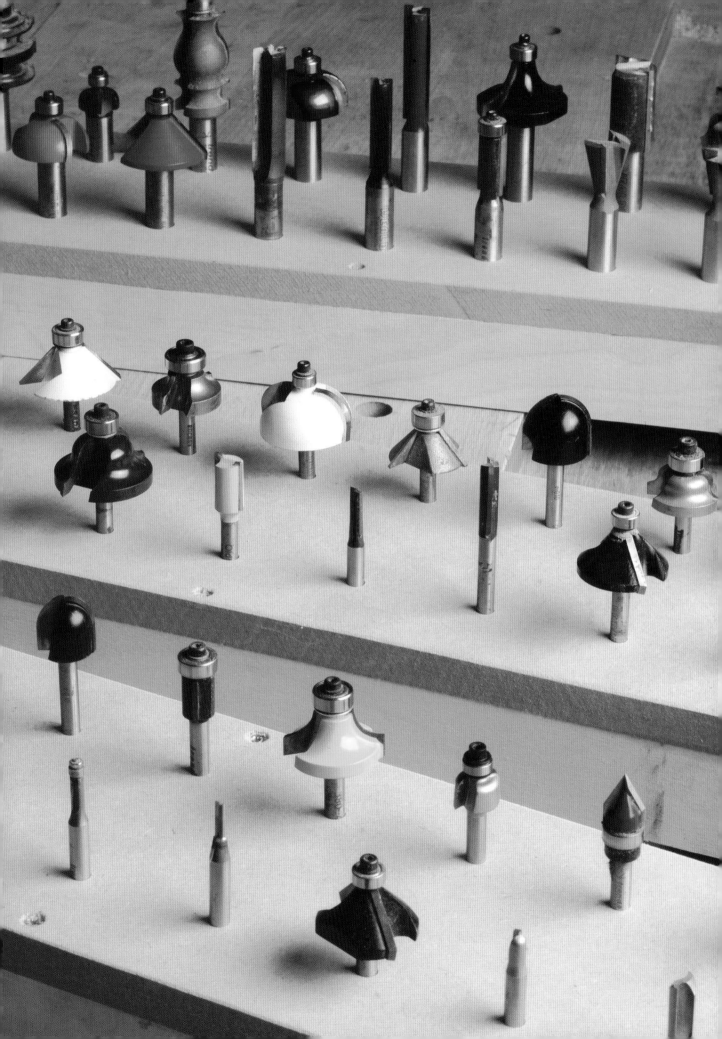

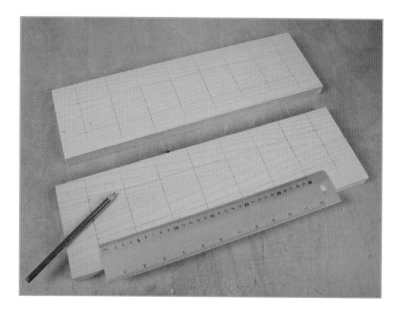

1 Find a suitable piece or pieces of 18mm-thick MDF, cut to size and mark out the cutter positions. I decided to make them 2in (50mm) apart widthwise, but with slightly deeper spacing from back to front so it was easier to lift any of the back row out for use.

2 Fit the straight cutter needed for the shank size required, e.g. ¼in for ¼in shank holes. Spraymount medium abrasive paper on the router base so the router stays still while you drill each hole. Set the depth of cut to about two-thirds of the board thickness. Aim the cutter carefully on each set of crossed lines in turn and plunge smoothly.

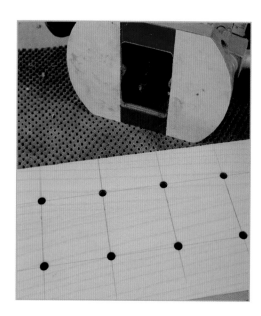

3 With care, the alignment of the holes should be very accurate. Slight scorching around the holes from drilling will easily sand away.

4 Sand all pencil marks away so the surface looks clean. Here, a board with ½in shank holes is being sanded to a finish.

5 Now glue two battens underneath. One will sit in the L-shape that we are going to fix to the wall; the other will keep the board level when it is taken down and sitting on the bench.

6 Make up an L-shape for the wall. The trick is to make the batten a fraction wider than those under the cutter board. That way the board will lift in and out easily. If you cannot machine it to the required size, use a strip of veneer as a packer to do the same thing. Drill and countersink ready for the screws.

7 Use one screw to fix the L-shape to the wall, check and adjust the level, then put screws in the other holes. There need to be enough screws to support the weight of the board when loaded with cutters.

★ WORKING TIP

Having made this excellent means of cutter storage, like all tools and cutters they will get dusty in the workshop. I decided to make a cabinet to keep these cutter selection boards in with a door that has a clear polycarbonate panel so I can see the cutters without even opening the door. When I need to, I can simply open the door and lift down the board with the cutters I want to use.

A finished cutter selection board.

TRAMMEL

Routers sometimes come with a trammel head that fits on a fence rod

for machining circular shapes – but not always. In any case, you might

want to make larger circles than such a set-up can manage.

This simple device allows you to cut circles with ease.

● **MATERIALS AND TOOLS**

- Offcut of 6mm MDF approx. 20½ x 4⁵⁄₁₆in (520 x 110mm)

- 6mm machine screw, two washers, nyloc nut and wingnut

- ¼in router cutter

- Two machine screws for router mounting

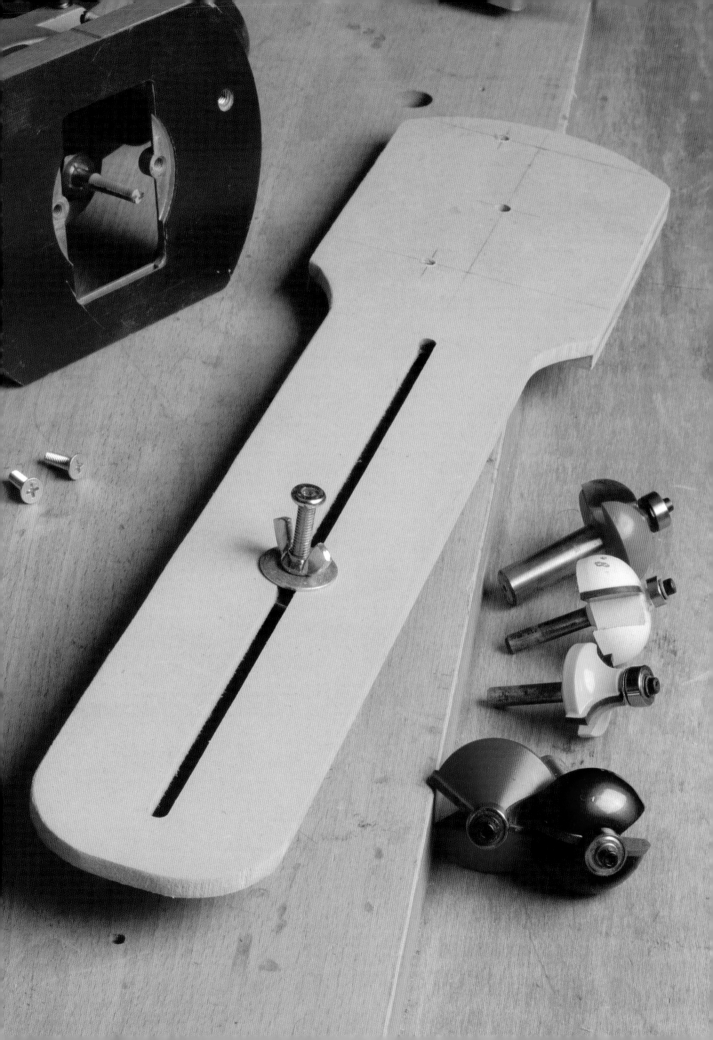

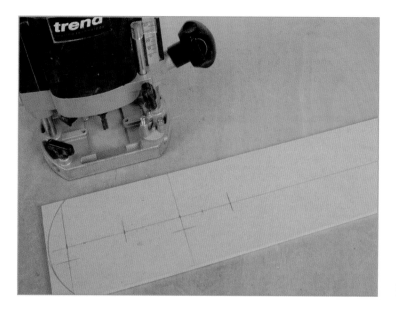

1 Mark out and cut your intended trammel board to size. You need a centreline and, at one end, the hole positions that match those on the router base. These are usually off the centreline – in this case the two small crosses towards the left-hand side. Also mark the edge of the router base and the limit of the slot the trammel point will move in.

2 Drill the holes for the machine screws that will mount the router. You need to countersink the holes on the underside so the heads sit in neatly.

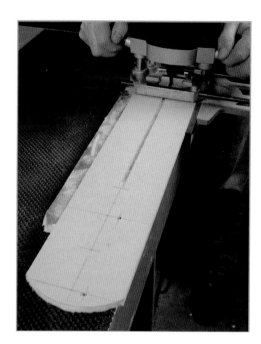

4 Cut the board down widthwise up to where the router will sit. This lightens the piece and makes it easier to see where you are working. All the curved edges need to be smoothed with a file or rasp.

3 Fix the trammel to a sacrificial surface with spray adhesive. I use polyurethane insulation board as it offers no resistance to the cutter and is easy to pull away once the job is done. Use the router and fence to make the trammel point slot down the middle, stopping short of both the router base area and the other end of the board.

5 Fix the router in place using the correct size machine screws.

6 In the slot, fit a 6mm machine screw that has been filed or ground to a point. A wingnut goes on first, then a large repair washer, then the 6mm MDF trammel, followed by another repair washer and finally a nyloc nut.

7 Glue two thin strips of 6mm MDF in place under the router base area. These will lift the trammel up just enough so the point and nyloc nut can project enough while keeping the trammel level.

8 To move the point along, simply undo the wingnut, slide the point along and tighten up the wingnut at the desired position. To fix the point in position, tap it with a hammer and press down on it while machining so the end cannot wander and ruin the workpiece.

★ WORKING TIP

I like to sharpen the tip of a trammel point but you don't have to do that. If you need to machine on the 'seen' face, then you may have to, but if you can use the trammel on the underside instead, you can just leave the machine screw square at the end. Simply drill a 'blind' hole the same diameter as the machine screw and make sure it extends far enough to rest properly in the hole before you start machining.

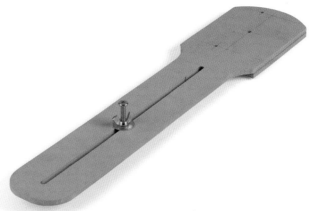

The finished trammel.

THICKNESS-SKIMMING JIG

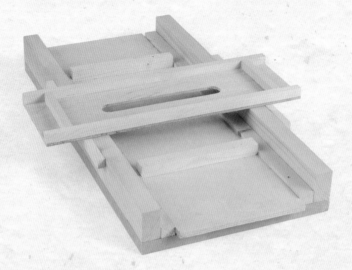

We don't all possess workshop machinery and, if you are new to routing, it is highly unlikely that you will have these resources available to you. Machines are big and expensive and yet if you want to reshape timber, you need a means of doing it. Softwood can easily be bought in prepared sections already planed, but hardwoods are often only sold in a sawn state; they may already be bowed out of shape, as hardwoods often misbehave as they dry out. A portable circular saw can be used for rough cutting, but you need to be able to flatten the faces of the timber. Here is a simple jig to help you do this.

● MATERIALS AND TOOLS

- Board offcut of 18mm MDF or ply to suit size of work

- Board offcut of 6mm ply to suit size of work

- Sections of softwood batten in various sizes

- PVA glue

- 1in (25mm) panel pins

- Hammer

- Try square

- Three-wing groundwork or bottom cutter

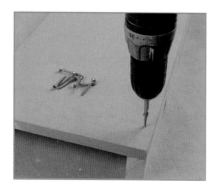

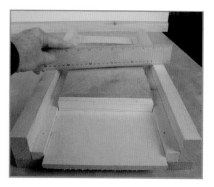

1 Choose a piece of 18mm MDF quite a bit wider than the intended workpieces. The length is less critical, as the workpiece can be moved along if necessary. Fix a batten along each side of the MDF and set exactly the same distance apart – use screws only, in case you need to make any changes to the design. The battens must be higher than the wood you need to skim.

2 The workpiece will probably need to sit on a thin ply sub-bed to bring it up close to the router. If it is short, pin a short fillet at each end to stop it sliding along.

3 Inside the battens you may need two fillets (a fillet is a smaller section than a batten). These will hold the workpiece and the sub-bed between the sides so they cannot move around. The fillets are lower than the workpieces you are going to skim flat; the router cutter will oversail them in use but stop short of the outer battens. Check that the mounted workpiece is slightly lower than the battens, as intended.

4 The correct type of cutter usually has three wings and rounded or bevelled corners to prevent dig-in. Their intended use if for groundwork machining, i.e, around carvings.

5 Make a long tray shape using 6mm-thick ply or MDF. This needs to be a bit wider than your router base and parallel. It should be somewhat longer than the width of the lower part of the jig it will be attached to so the router cutter can oversail it safely. A straight-sided router base is much easier to make this tray for, although it will still work with a circular or one-flat-side type. Glue and clamp a small fillet along one side of the tray base. Once dry, press the router base against it and glue and clamp the other fillet against it. Slide the router along and check that it is a good sliding fit all the way along. Remove the router and wipe off any excess glue from the tray and the router base so there is no

interference when you use it later. To complete the tray shape, glue two short fillets at the ends of the tray to stop the travel of the router. It is important that the cutter cannot go far enough to cut into the battens, so check that the fillets will stop the travel at the right place. This tray will slide backwards and forwards along the jig so it needs two fillets glued in place underneath that sit outside the battens on the lower part of the jig. To make the movement of the tray as smooth as possible, these fillets should be longer than the width of the tray they are attached to. This has the effect of increasing the running surface and preventing the tray from jiggling from side to side as you push and pull it.

8 This close view of a part-machined board shows just how parallel and flat a result you can achieve. I was surprised how good it was the first time I tried it, and it is well worth using this jig if you have no other means of thicknessing.

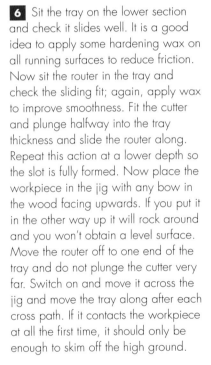

6 Sit the tray on the lower section and check it slides well. It is a good idea to apply some hardening wax on all running surfaces to reduce friction. Now sit the router in the tray and check the sliding fit; again, apply wax to improve smoothness. Fit the cutter and plunge halfway into the tray thickness and slide the router along. Repeat this action at a lower depth so the slot is fully formed. Now place the workpiece in the jig with any bow in the wood facing upwards. If you put it in the other way up it will rock around and you won't obtain a level surface. Move the router off to one end of the tray and do not plunge the cutter very far. Switch on and move it across the jig and move the tray along after each cross path. If it contacts the workpiece at all the first time, it should only be enough to skim off the high ground.

7 Repeat this operation at a lower depth, removing just a millimetre at a time, and continue until the entire surface has been skimmed flat. Now turn the workpiece over and repeat the whole operation. Use a thicker packer if necessary, as the workpiece will now be thinner and therefore lower than when you started.

★ **WORKING TIP**

Some operations, such as thickness skimming, can produce a lot of chippings and dust that need proper extraction. Always use the router's own extraction pipe connected to an extractor. If you can add another pipe close to the workpiece so much the better, otherwise detach the hose between passes and use it to clear all the waste material so you can see what you are doing and keep the mess to a minimum.

The finished thickness-skimming jig.

SHELF-TYPE ROUTER TABLE

Although I make a lot of jigs and work aids, I love simplicity; one of my greatest satisfactions is proving how easy and cheap it can be to make something. This super-easy router table is a great example. I needed to make one in a hurry once, when I was forced to stay at home during a snowy winter but also needed to carry on working and I didn't have a router table to hand. It took me five minutes to make, but I'll let you take a little longer – say ten minutes?

● MATERIALS AND TOOLS

- Offcut of 15mm melamine-faced board 19¾ x 15in (500 x 380mm)

- Offcut of 3 x 2in (75 x 50mm) softwood PAR batten 19¾ (500mm) long

- Tenon saw

- Several smaller drill bits

- Countersink

- Machine screws to fit router base holes

- NVR switch

- Fine height adjuster

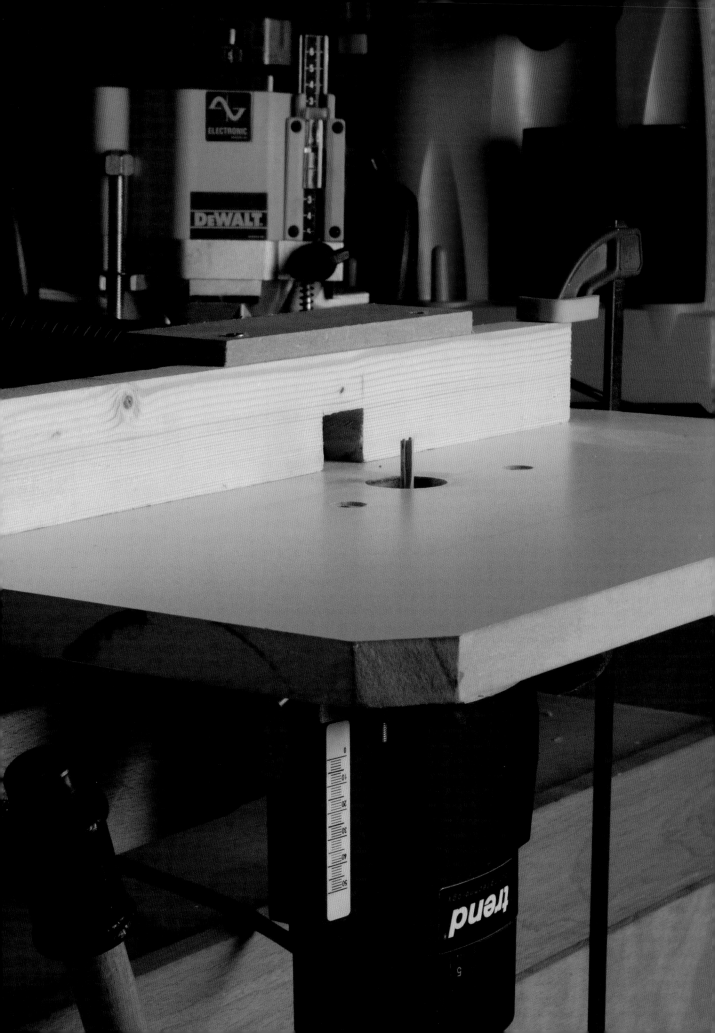

1 Choose a piece of melamine-faced MDF for the table surface and cut it to a convenient size. I have suggested dimensions, but do whatever you can with the board available.

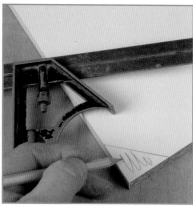

2 Nip off the two front corners with a handsaw or chopsaw and sand all the edges so they are smooth and comfortable to the touch.

3 Around the middle of the board, mark the hole positions for mounting your router. Almost all routers have mounting holes; these tend to be an identical distance apart.

4 Drill the mounting holes, ensuring they are the same size or slightly larger than the machine screws that will be used to fix the router in position.

5 Countersink the holes so the heads of the machine's screws sit just below the top surface and cannot interfere with the workpieces that will be fed across the table.

6 Screw a batten underneath near the back for vice mounting; alternatively, you can bolt it down if you have long enough bolts.

7 Fix the table in position and mount the router with a straight cutter installed, checking that it fits tightly under the table. You may need shorter or longer bolts if it doesn't mount properly.

8 Take a piece of straight batten for a fence. Cut out a cutter recess in the middle and clamp it in place with quick clamps.

■ FINISHING OFF

Your table is complete and ready to use. There are three final steps to consider, however:

1 You need extraction; this can simply be a workshop vacuum-cleaner hose clamped to the table behind the fence.

2 Fit an NVR (No Volt Release) switch for your safety so you don't fiddle around under the table trying to find the router's own switch, and so you have emergency shut-off should you need it.

3 You need a fine-height adjuster or it will be impossible to raise and lower the router (although some models come with this fitted).

★ WORKING TIP

It doesn't matter what size hole you make in the table but you might as well make it as large as you are likely to need, so a 19mm straight cutter is a good choice. It will also give plenty of room for the bearing on a guided cutter to rise up through the table when you need to use that type of cutter.

The finished shelf-type router table.

LARGE ROUTER TABLE

Once you realize how useful a router table is, you may be tempted to make a larger and more sophisticated one. This table incorporates features you would normally only get on a commercial table. I only use good-quality birch ply for a job like this, assembled with a biscuit jointer or biscuit cutter in a freehand router. A waste piece of laminate sheet has been used on the tabletop and fence, bonded down with contact adhesive. A high-quality table insert plate and mitre protractor guide track have been fitted into machined recesses, and there are special insert nuts fitted in the tabletop and fence for fixing the fence and accessories to the table.

● MATERIALS AND TOOLS

- One and a half standard 8 x 4ft (2,440 x 1,220mm) boards of 18mm birch ply

- 9mm birch ply

- PVA glue

- White melamine laminate sheet for tabletop and fence front

- Thixotropic contact adhesive

- 1¼in (30mm) and 1½in (40mm) twinfast screws

- Size 20 biscuits

- Table insert

- NVR switch

- 4 x 2½in (65mm) hinges

- 2 x rare earth magnet door closers

- 12.7mm straight cutter

- 6.4mm straight cutter

- Bevel cutter

- Various table fittings: knobs, nuts, anchor bolts, bolts, washers

DIMENSIONAL DIAGRAM

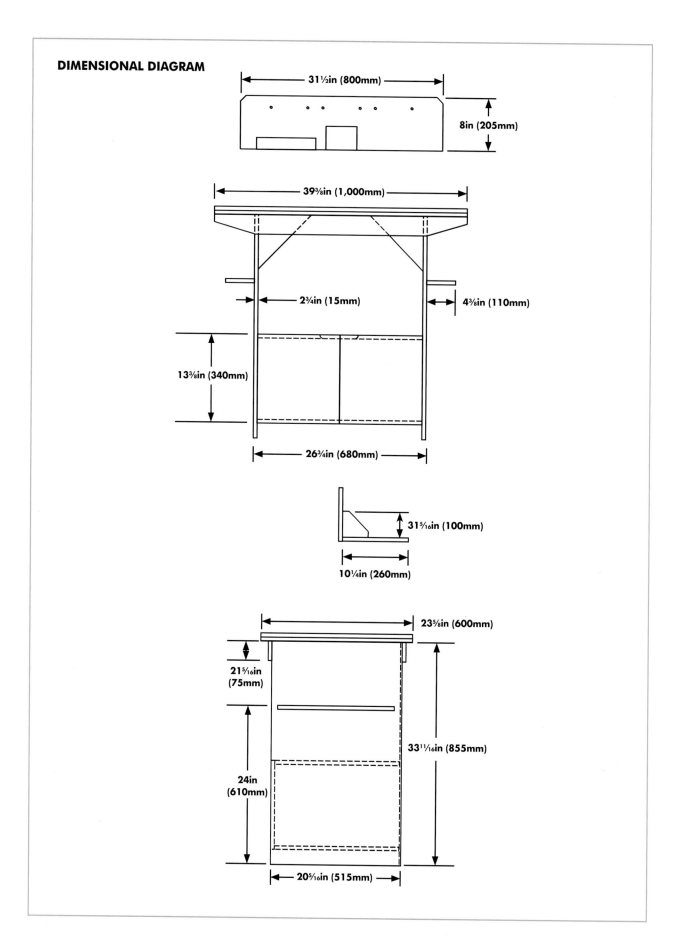

◆ TABLE CUTTING LIST

18mm birch ply:

Top 39⅜ x 23⅝in (1,000 x 600mm) x 2

Sides 33¹¹⁄₁₆ x 20⁵⁄₁₆in (855 x 515mm) x 2

Shelves 25⅜ x 19¼in (644 x 488mm) x 2

Top supports 39⅜ x 3in (1,000 x 75mm) x 2

Cutter shelves 18 x 4⅜in (455 x 110mm) x 2

Brackets Cut from 8¼in-wide board (210mm) x 4

Doors 13⅜ x 12¹¹⁄₁₆in (340 x 322mm) x 2

Back panel Approx. 33¹¹⁄₁₆ x 20⅜ x ¼in (approx. 855 x 670mm x 6mm) x 1

◆ FENCE CUTTING LIST

18mm birch ply:

Fence front 31½ x 8in (800 x 205mm) x 1

Fence base 31½ x 10¼in (800 x 260mm) x 1

Brackets From 18mm offcuts

Dust enclosure 6mm birch ply offcuts

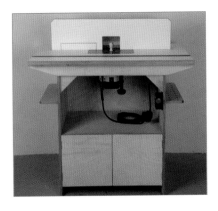

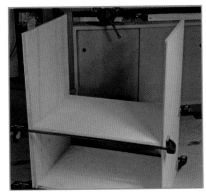

1 The finished table looks like a piece of highly functional cabinet furniture. The short shelves underneath the table are drilled with a router to store cutters. The doors have the hinges fully recessed into them, not the carcass. Rare earth magnets hold the doors closed, and there are neatly recessed door pulls on the top edges. The open area around the router is easily cleared of chippings with a vacuum and an NVR is fitted at the right-hand side. A homemade fine adjuster using a box spanner and a plastic knob allow precise height setting.

2 The carcass construction is very simple: two sides and two shelves screwed and biscuited together. The screw heads should be sunk in counterbored holes so the holes can then be plugged with a contrast timber.

3 The front top rail can be either tongue-and-grooved or biscuited; it can be slid into place after the carcass has been assembled. The back panel is thin birch ply set in a rebate on the back of the carcass.

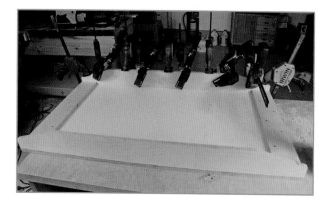

4 The birch ply top has a laminate on both faces to keep it stable. Then the front and back support rails are fixed to it and the flat strip screwed in place underneath the ends to make it completely rigid. The support rails are spaced exactly apart so they fit neatly over the carcass.

5 You will need an insert plate to carry the router. There are several types on the market; each comes with fitting instructions that are correct to that particular plate. You will need to accurately locate and mount your router. Usually this involves removing the baseplate facing and using it as a template for drilling the plate.

6 The plate neatly installed in the tabletop. It needs to be exactly flush with the surface with no gaps around it. Note the two insert nuts at the rear of the table ready to take the fence.

7 This insert place does not sit on a rebate as some do. Instead, the manufacturer provides special corner mountings onto which the plate is screwed down. They also incorporate height adjustment so you can get the plate exactly flush to the table surface for smooth running over. Note the mitre guide track, which has been let into a wide routed groove.

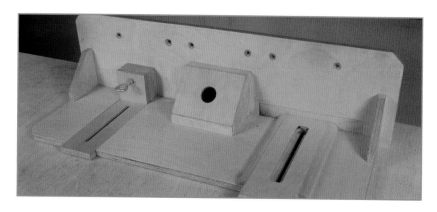

8 The rear view of the fence showing fine fence adjustment at the left and adjustable outfeed support at the right. Star knobs complete with machine threads lock the fence onto the table. There are no fewer than six insert nuts for mounting various accessories. At the outfeed side is an adjustable fence section to give support when the face of a workpiece has been machined away.

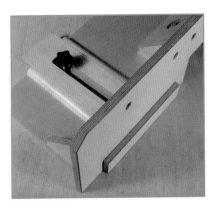

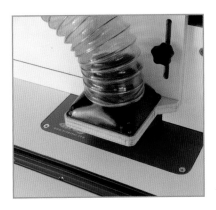

9 A view of the outfeed support showing how it can be moved forward (the degree of extension has been exaggerated for clarity).

10 The fine fence adjustment can still be operated when the fence is locked in position. The eyebolt runs through several nuts; the ones in the block at the front have thread-locking compound applied so the bolt can still turn in the hole without them tightening up.

11 A combined extraction port and hold-down ensures that chippings are removed efficiently. It is connected to a large, powerful drum extractor.

12 Here are several other accessories you can make: spring fingers (top left) for safe working, including one that sits in the mitre track (bottom), and a tunnel (top right) for safe, easy machining of very small sections.

The finished large router table.

★ **WORKING TIP**

Sand all surfaces before final assembly and apply a quick-dry, water-based varnish to seal them.

BOARD-CUTTING FACILITY

From time to time you will need to cut out material from large manufactured boards such as ply or MDF. Generally these are 8 x 4ft (2,440 x 1,220mm), although 10 x 5ft (3,050 x 1,525mm) boards are also available. We will concentrate on the former size, as this is more common. The arrangement I have described here is not unique or very difficult to make – it is just a common-sense solution. There are less sturdy supports on the market, but this solution won't let you down!

● MATERIALS AND TOOLS

- PAR softwood

- Piece of 9mm MDF

- 6in (150mm) nails

- 4in (100mm) twinfast screws

- Hardpoint handsaw or portable circular saw

- 16mm stagger-tooth or pocket cutter (½in shank)

- Chamfer cutter

- ½in shank heavy-duty router for mortising, complete with guide bush

- Heavy claw hammer

- Sharp 1½in (38mm) chisel

◆ **CUTTING LIST**

All lengths shown are at finished size, but allow a bit extra for trimming:

Top rails 42 × 6 × 2in (1080 × 150 × 50mm) × 4

Ends 24 × 8 × 2in (605 × 200 × 50mm) × 4

Bottom rails 36 × 6 × 2in (910 × 150 × 50mm) × 2

Feet 15¾ × 4 × 2in (400 × 100 × 50mm) × 4

Support bars 86½ × 3 × 2in (2200 × 75 × 50mm) × 3

DIMENSIONAL DIAGRAM

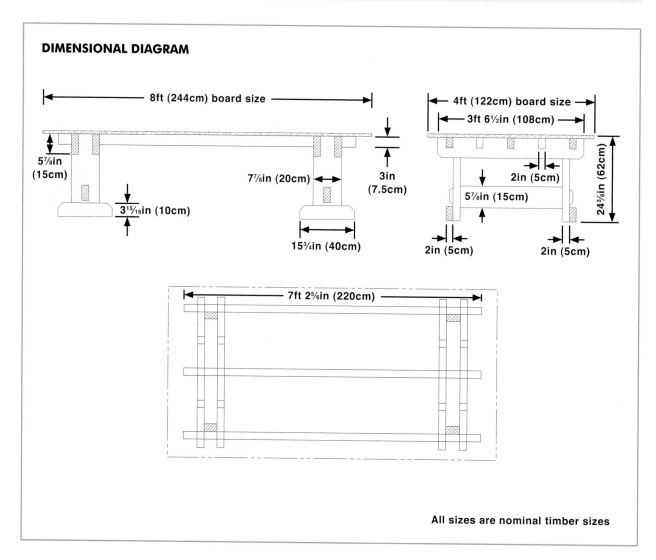

All sizes are nominal timber sizes

1 The set-up must hold 8 × 4ft (2,440 × 1,220mm) sheets. It must hold them flat and you must be able to put the whole thing away so that it doesn't take up precious space. The answer would seem to be a modified sawhorse. Sawhorses in pairs give good work support to long timber and don't take up much space when stacked. However, they don't cope so well with boards that can be thin or heavy and prone to sag. The traditional sawhorse also needs to be made correctly, and involves compound angles for the top, which has to be notched out to take the legs. There is a bit of skill in putting this basic piece of carpentry kit together.

2 As an alternative, I have designed a sawhorse that is much easier to make and works perfectly well. Two of them won't interlock on top of each other, but you can stand one on top of the other for storage. Note how these horses are rather longer than usual – they will give adequate support to the board crosswise, although they are not intended to span the entire width. A key feature of this set-up is the slots in each sawhorse, which take the lengthwise support rails.

3 All the top surfaces are level with each other, and when a full board is placed in the middle there is room all round for cramping a straightedge in place. The additional slots allow you to move the support rails over when you are working with narrower boards. You could of course fit some kind of box underneath to carry bits and pieces, but it will need a lid or it will soon fill up with dust and chips. This set-up works well for home use or for professional routing on-site.

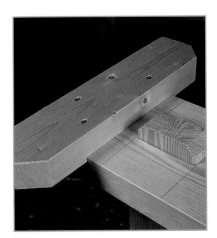

4 This model has the further advantage of being cheap to make, because it only needs standard prepared softwood.

★ **WORKING TIP**

Modern twinfast screws can make quick work of assembling softwood structures but you need to take a little care. It pays to pre-drill clearance holes in the top component and to countersink those holes unless the screws you use are designed to self-countersink. It is less important to drill pilot holes in the underneath component as it is less likely to split when screwing the two pieces together. Set the drill's torque ring so the screw heads just set in below the surface of the wood.

The finished board-cutting facility.

PROJECTS
FOR THE HOME

SHELVES

Sometimes you don't need a whole wall full of self-assembly-type shelves. Instead, you might just want a small set of shelves that have a pleasing traditional style and can be a feature on the wall. In that case, this design may be just what you are looking for. It uses prepared softwood board and a length of cornice that is split on the table saw to create the lower-stage moulding.

● MATERIALS AND TOOLS

- Softwood PAR boards
- Softwood cornice
- Medium abrasive sheet and disc

- PVA glue
- ¼in straight cutter
- Rebate cutter

- Bottom-bearing-guided cutter
- Jigsaw or bandsaw
- Hammer and punch

DIMENSIONAL DIAGRAM

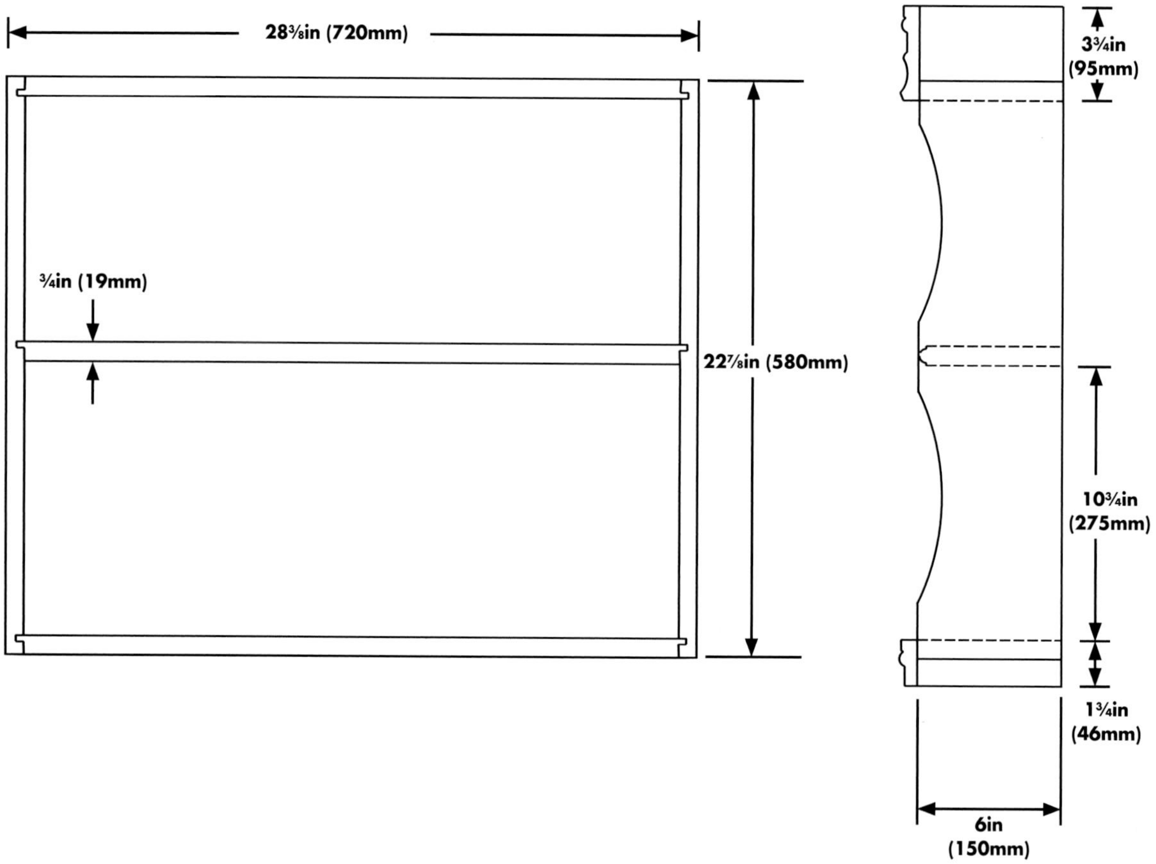

28⅜in (720mm)

¾in (19mm)

22⅞in (580mm)

3¾in (95mm)

10¾in (275mm)

1¾in (46mm)

6in (150mm)

◆ **CUTTING LIST**

Shelves Approx. 28⅜ x 6 x ¾in (approx. 720 x 150 x 19mm) x 3

Ends 22⅞ x 6 x ¾in (580 x 150 x 19mm) x 2

Top moulding Approx. 3¾in (95mm) high, long enough for front and ends

Bottom moulding Approx. 1¾in (46mm) high, long enough for front and ends

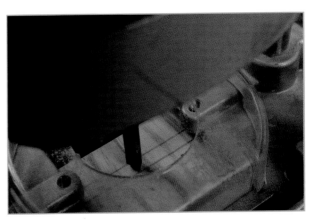

1 Mark out the top and bottom of the carcass and the shelf in the middle, which is set slightly higher up. This looks better and suits different-sized books or objects. Note the slots marked that will be machined in the carcass sides to take the shelf tongues.

2 Clamp a router T-square on the carcass to machine each slot in turn, making sure the cutter lines up with the pencil lines.

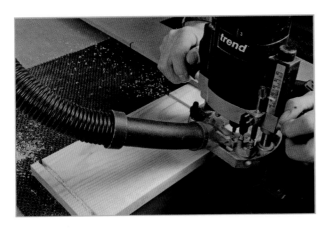

3 Machine each slot in two passes to depth so as not to strain the cutter. The slots in both carcass sides should line up accurately together.

4 The shelves all have tongues machined on the ends. The fit in the slots must be tight, especially as softwood fibres crush easily and the joints may therefore loosen a bit. Do test cuts first to get the correct fit, making sure the tongues are no deeper than the slots.

5 Find a suitable shape to draw a curve between the shelf positions. If necessary, move the shape and redraw until it looks right. Leave a short straight section at each end leading up to the shelves.

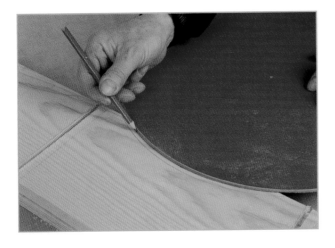

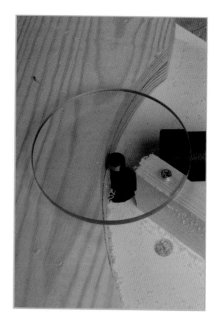

6 Bandsaw the curves out accurately on one shelf side. Use a spokeshave or wood rasp to even the curve and then use abrasive paper to finish it off.

7 Lay the first shelf side on the other and draw the curves on it. Cut it away from the line by ⅛in (2–3mm). Now pin one side on top of the other side.

8 Fit a bottom-bearing-guided cutter in a table-mounted router. Place a guard over the top and have an extraction pipe close by. Run the bearing against the already shaped side piece so the cutter copies the cut on the other one.

9 Now fit a roundover cutter in the table and machine the front edges of the shelf sides. Do this from both faces and with it set so it creates a slight step effect. You may need to plug the shelf slots temporarily if the bearing is likely to slip into them and spoil the cut.

10 Repeat this procedure on the middle shelf front edge, this time using the table fence set level with the cutter bearing.

11 Sand all the components and then glue and assemble them. Clamp carefully so all the tongue-and-groove joints close properly, and check that the whole thing is square. The best way is to measure both diagonals. These should be identical; if not, adjust the clamps until it is square.

12 Mitre the top moulding accurately and glue and pin it around the top of the bookcase using a pencil line to guide where the moulding should be. Use a punch to sink the pin heads. Repeat this operation on the lower moulding, which hangs down. Once the mouldings are fitted, fill the holes carefully and sand the filler away when dry. Lastly, apply a few coats of water-based clear varnish to seal and make it shine.

★ WORKING TIP

Although this book is all about routing there is nothing to say you shouldn't buy ready-made mouldings and incorporate them in projects. They give you access to different profiles and it saves buying an expensive cutter and needing a large router when you only want to do one job. The cornice moulding used in this project is a good example as it has several stages to it that cannot be replicated except with a special cutter. However, as shown elsewhere in this book, you can also build up profiles from several thicknesses of pre-machined components.

The finished shelves.

BEDSIDE CABINET

I was lucky with this project; I had some large ply boards with a dark satin finish already applied, so I cut it up to make this bedside cabinet. You will need to make up the bare wood cabinet and apply a finish once it is assembled. This is an exercise in making a square carcass, adding solid lippings all round to cover the ply edges and then adding roundover detail where necessary.

● MATERIALS AND TOOLS

- 18mm ply

- 6mm ply

- Prepared hardwood sections for lippings

- Size 20 biscuits

- PVA glue

- Medium and fine abrasives

- Dark satin wood finish

- Biscuit cutter

- 4mm straight cutter

- 6.4mm straight cutter

- Hinge mortising cutter

- 9.5mm-radius roundover cutter

- 2 x 50mm brass hinges

- Cupboard catch

- Brass handle

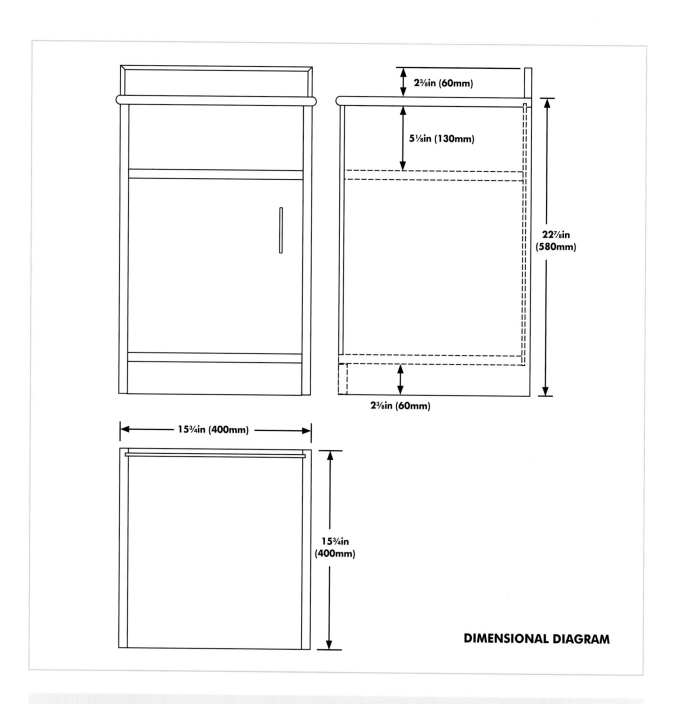

DIMENSIONAL DIAGRAM

2⅜in (60mm)

5⅛in (130mm)

22⅞in (580mm)

2⅜in (60mm)

15¾in (400mm)

15¾in (400mm)

◆ **CUTTING LIST**

18mm ply:

Top 15¾ × 15¾in (400 × 400mm) × 1

Sides 22⅞ × 15¹⁄₁₆in (580 × 380mm) × 2

Shelves 14⁵⁄₁₆ × 14¾in (364 × 374mm) × 2

Upstand 15¹⁄₁₆ × 2in (380 × 50mm) × 1

Plinth 14⁵⁄₁₆ × 2⅜in (364 × 60mm) × 1

Door 14⁵⁄₁₆ × 13¾in (364 × 350mm) × 1

Back panel Approx. 23¼ × 15⅜ × ¼in (approx. 590 × 390 × 6mm) × 1

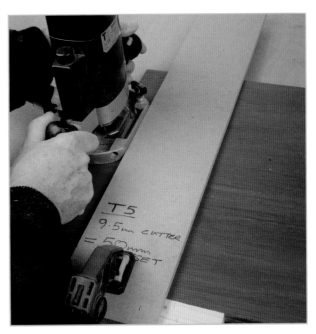

1 All the parts are cut to size apart from the door and the thin ply back panel, which will be trimmed to fit later on. Use a fine-tooth blade to give a clear cut and minimize tearout.

2 Clean up all sawn edges using a router with a 19mm-diameter straight cutter and a T-square. Make sure components match each other where necessary. It is better to trim slightly so they are compatible with each other at assembly time.

3 Mark the T-square with biscuit slot positions. You can then use it for repeatable setting out and machining. It is particularly useful for the mid-panel slots needed for the middle and lower shelves.

4 Mark the mid-panel slot position and use a 4mm straight cutter to create the biscuit slots. Check the length of a size 20 biscuit and make the slots slightly longer. Remember that the shelves that joint to them must have matching edge slots and that the slots should be centred in the thickness of the boards.

5 Use the marks on the T-square to mark the edge slot positions. It is better to keep them close together for strength.

6 Having marked the centre of each slot, make a mark either side of it so you can see where to start and finish the slot. A little experimentation is needed to decide this. Remember to enter and exit the workpiece from the side; do not unplunge the router as the cutter will damage the slot.

7 Draw where the bottom shelf will go and repeat the biscuiting operation as before. The plinth section at the front also requires biscuits to fix it in position.

8 Now do a dry assembly to ensure that everything fits together properly. Use pincers to remove the biscuits cleanly afterwards.

9 Mount the router in the router table and fit a 6.4mm straight cutter to make the back panel grooves in the two carcass sides.

10 Check again that everything fits correctly with the back panel in position. It is better to identify problems before gluing up.

11 Now apply glue to biscuit slots in one meeting surface and loosely fit the biscuits. Run glue all along the opposite meeting surfaces and mate the joints together. Start by fitting the shelves to the sides including the plinth; put the top on last. Use a hammer and block to line components together, then clamp firmly and wipe off the surplus glue. Check the carcass is square.

12 Glue and tape solid lippings in position. These should be the same thickness as the ply and be carefully placed with surfaces flush. Trim off surplus length using a very fine-toothed saw.

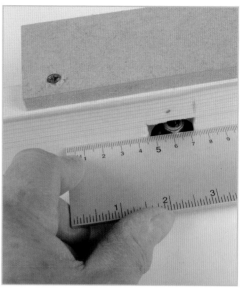

13 The upstand at the back needs to be biscuited in position and then the lippings mitred to fit and glued on. It is easier to cut the mitres to butt neatly first, then trim the square ends afterwards as that is easier to do. This technique can be used on all the lippings on this cabinet.

14 The top has a square section lipping applied, which needs to be rounded over on the front edges. Set up a roundover cutter in the table and adjust the fence so it is in line with the bearing.

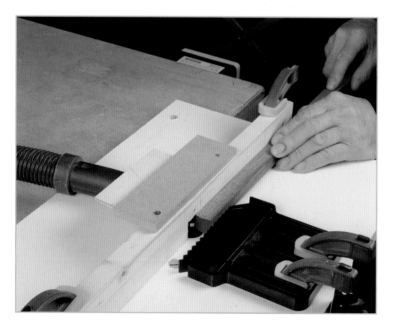

15 Proceed to mould sufficient lengths of wood to do the job. Make sure you use pressure fingers to avoid vibration and make the operation safer.

16 The carcass is now complete apart from the back panel.

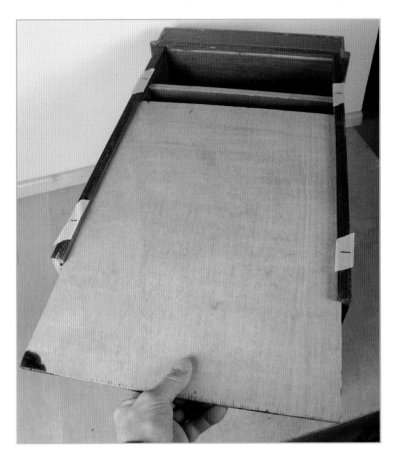

18 Cut the door to size, then edge it with iron-on veneer tape or make the door smaller and glue a solid lipping on. Trim the door to fit so there is a slight but equal gap all round. Put a 12.7mm straight or hinge mortise cutter in the router, plunge it at rest and place a hinge under the depth rod at the thinnest part so you can set the correct recess depth.

17 Mark on some tape where the shelves are so you know where to pin, then slide the back panel in and use hammer and pins to fix it securely.

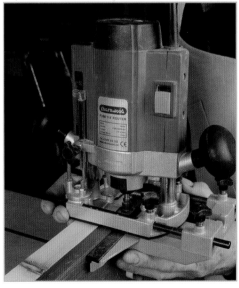

19 Clamp a longer board alongside the door flush with the top so the router will run smoothly with good support. Make the first cut a shallow pre-scoring cut. This will avoid the wood tearing out.

20 Loosen the fence and move the router over to do a full-width cut. Note the low hand grip, which helps to hold it steady and pressed against the door.

21 Square out both recesses with a sharp chisel and clean the bottom of the cut with the chisel laying flat.

22 The hinge should be a neat fit. The pencil lines on the batten were a visual guide for routing, as they would not show up on the dark surface and would mar it.

23 Drill and carefully fit the screws. The heads must be small enough to go flush into the surface of the hinge leaf. Because the hinges are fully recessed into the door, they are surface-mounted in the carcass without recessing them. Set the door back slightly from the carcass front edge as it will look neater.

24 The opening side of the door will need a stop to press against. Pin a small fillet of wood for the door to touch against. Put a pin in the middle, close the door firmly and it will line the fillet correctly. Now pin near each end.

25 Fit the handle and ball catch. The ball catch requires a hole drilled that is the correct diameter; tap it home with a hammer.

26 Once the applied finish has dried, use fine wirewool followed by wax to impart a soft sheen to the surfaces.

■ RECYCLING TIMBER

I am extremely careful with wood. There is no point in wasting a precious resource that costs money. I made this project with panels retrieved from a previous project and which I had kept stored. I have a regime for timber and board recovery. For DIY projects as opposed to cabinetmaking, I use top-quality twinfast screws that I know won't burr over when driven in so I can remove them easily and are reuseable. Likewise I try to avoid filling over screwheads and minimize the use of glue to allow for quick disassembly.

Where nails, glue and damaged screws make a construct hard to take apart, I try and 'flatpack' it by removing any back panels and squashing it flat, then once it has fallen apart I saw off any sections with metal buried or awkward lumps of timber that won't separate. This leaves me with reusable panels that stack easily. This also applies to lengths of recovered softwood, although buried metal partway along is not necessarily a problem so long as I mark where it is. All the awkward unusable sections of timber remaining are then cut down to very short lengths on the bandsaw, metal and all, with any nails hammered flat if they won't pull out. These pieces are stacked ready for winter and my woodburning stove.

The finished bedside cabinet.

STOOL

A stool is a handy thing to have around, when you need an impromptu extra seat or the kids want somewhere to sit. There are some interesting techniques involved, but nothing you cannot achieve with a bit of thought and preparation. I chose beech because it is a light wood, but it is also quite tough and hardwearing and finishes well. A stool is very usable, doesn't take up much room and is not as complex as making a chair, for instance.

● MATERIALS AND TOOLS

- Prepared oak (see cutting list on page 196 for dimensions)

- 6mm MDF strip

- Softwood batten

- 6.4mm straight cutter

- Guide bush

- Small and medium roundover cutters

- PVA glue

- Abrasives

DIMENSIONAL DIAGRAM

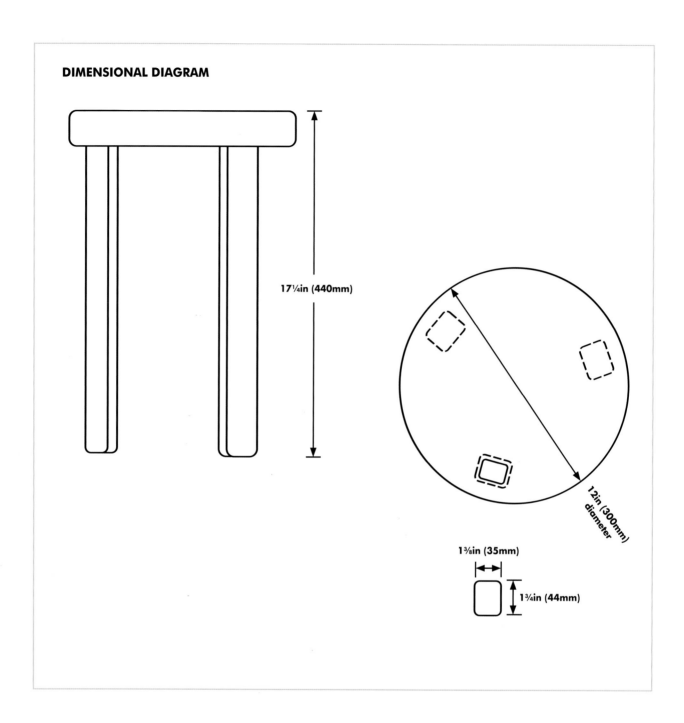

17¼in (440mm)

12in (300mm) diameter

1⅜in (35mm)

1¾in (44mm)

◆ **CUTTING LIST**

A short board of prepared oak producing:

Seat 12in diameter x 1¾in (300mm diameter x 44mm) x 1

Legs Approx. 17 x 1¾ x 1⅜in (approx. 430 x 44 x 35mm) x 3

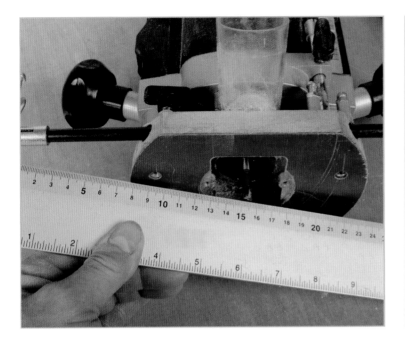

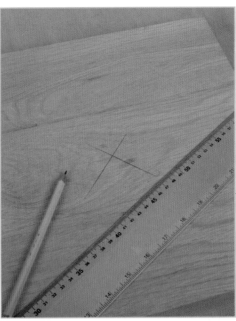

1 The stool seat has to be made first. Fit a trammel to your router, either one that came with it or make one as shown in the project on pp. 154–157. Measure and set it so it will cut a 12in (300mm)-diameter circle. If the timber is not wide enough you will need to plane and glue two boards together first.

2 Mark the diagonals so you can find the centre. This ensures you will be able to machine a complete circle without running over the edge.

3 Tap the trammel end so the point bites into the wood slightly. This will be the underside, so a small hole will not matter.

4 Fit extraction as the chippings will be prodigious. Hold the trammel point down and machine a complete circle at a shallow pass. When you have done one complete circle, unplunge and move the router back to the start again. That will ensure the hose and cable do not get wound up tight. It will take a number of passes to reach full depth; don't rush it as it will strain the cutter.

5 When you have plunged as far as possible you almost certainly will not have gone through the full board thickness. This is nothing to worry about – routing has an answer!

6 First bandsaw away the waste, leaving a slight overhang that will be removed in the next operation.

7 Set up the router table with a bottom-bearing-guided cutter. Use a lead-in pin as a safe start-off point and then machine all around the seat. Check the bearing is running against the smooth upper section. The result is a perfect smooth-sided circle.

8 The next step is to make the leg mortises. This must be done before rounding over the seat edges as it gives a good edge against which to line up a jig. Choose the cutter and guide bush combination; preferably a 6.4mm straight cutter and a guide bush of 16mm diameter. Mark out the mortise size on a strip of MDF and then the guide bush allowance around it.

9 Machine the outer rectangle using a straight fence on the opposite side to the cut to avoid spoiling the cut as you will only run into the waste area. Use a sacrificial board underneath. I like to use a piece of polyurethane insulation board as it offers no resistance to the cutter.

10 The crosswise cuts need to be done running against a T-square clamped in place. If you do not overrun the corners you will end up with a very neat opening.

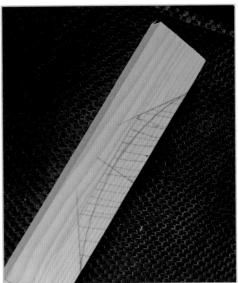

11 The mortise jig needs a fence, but of course we need three legs around a circular shape. First mark the curve on a piece of batten.

12 Now mark a line parallel to the edge that is slightly clear of the drawn curve. Then draw a two-angled line at the sides again clear of the curve.

13 Cut out the shape thus created. You will see that just the two outer bevelled corners rest on the seat. These will ensure it fits properly against any part of the curve.

14 Glue and clamp the strip of MDF onto the fence. It is important to make sure the fence is perpendicular to the batten. Check this with a try square on the outer face of the fence, which of course is flat. Wipe off surplus glue and leave it to dry.

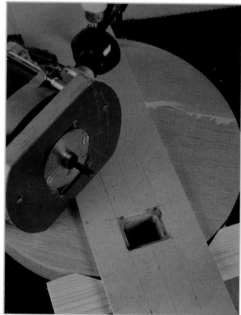

15 Mark the three axes on which the mortises will lie. You can do this by stepping out the three divisions with a large pair of dividers or a fillet with a nail as a point at one end and a pencil at the other. Clamp the jig on one axis at the far end away from the router.

16 Make the first mortise machine at successive depths; make sure you do not machine too far and risk breaking though the other side. You will need to clear the hole with an extractor as it will block with chippings and not allow you to machine right into the corners.

17 The three mortises completed successfully. Note that some filler was used where there was a large defect in the wood. After another sanding, the remaining filler can be dyed to blend in, although it won't normally be visible underneath the stool.

18 Mark the tenons and machine them on the router table with a square push-block behind for support. Increase the height of the cutter and turn the leg over; repeat until you get a good push fit into the mortise at an angle.

19 Repeat the operation for the two narrow edges and again check the fit by pushing into the mortise at an angle.

20 Use a bevelled 45° push-block to remove the corners so the tenons will fit properly in the holes. Rest the leg on it and raise the cutter until it cuts a small bevel on the tenon. Repeat on all corners and raise the cutter slightly more if necessary until the tenon fits comfortably.

21 The legs need a small roundover. This is done against the straight fence using a bearing-guided roundover cutter with the bearing set flush with the fence. This small 3.2mm roundover gives a perfect finish to the edges and is very quick and easy to apply in one pass. Do some test cuts to ensure you get the full profile without leaving a ridge where the cutter is set too high.

22 The leg ends are done in the same way but with a push-block behind to keep them square. The ends are equally easy to do so long as you hold it squarely against the pushblock. The corners will need rounding with a file or abrasive paper.

23 A larger roundover cutter is fitted in the table; both edges of the seat can now be rounded. Remember to push the seat against the direction of cutter rotation and do not falter or burning of the wood grain may occur.

24 The seat surfaces are sanded smooth including blending the edge curves in with the flat surfaces. Use a swinging over wrist action if using an orbital sander, otherwise a sheet of abrasive paper on a cork sanding block will do equally well.

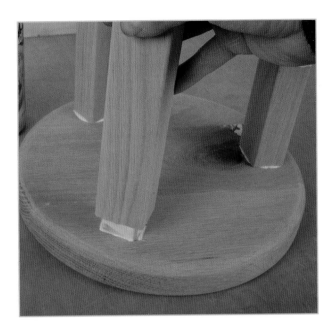

25 Apply PVA glue to the tenons and push them home into the mortises. Check that the legs are square and wipe off any surplus glue. Be careful to spread the glue evenly on the tenon faces and edges so that not too much gets pushed back out or else the joint may not be properly glued.

26 When the piece is dry, apply a couple of coats of spray lacquer in an open, ventilated area. This will seal the wood ready for wirewooling and waxing. It is a good idea to use fine-grade grey finishing paper between coats as it will cut down any dust or 'nibs' on the surface and give a better result after the second coat of lacquer.

■ USING FINISHES

Generally wood needs a finish applied to toughen the surface and make it suitable for its particular use.

Spray aerosol lacquer was used on this stool but it is highly volatile and flammable. It must be used in a very well-ventilated area (outdoor is best) and preferably using a lightweight organic filter mask to make the air safer to breathe. There must be no naked lights or sparks and the lacquer should be applied in light coats to avoid sags and runs.

Oil finishes such as Danish oil are very good but take longer between coats, and surplus oil must be removed as it will go very sticky on the surface otherwise. The rags used must be laid spread out outdoors after use because they pose an oxidation hazard, i.e. they may catch fire – this is a very real risk.

The finished stool.

FLAT-SCREEN MEDIA CENTRE

This is the biggest project in the book. This media unit is designed to be a height
that makes a flat-screen TV comfortable to watch when mounted on the wall above.
There is also plenty of drawer space for DVDs and so on. If you have extra equipment,
it can sit under the screen with speakers to either side. This piece is light
in appearance so it won't overpower its surroundings.

MATERIALS AND TOOLS

- Board and half of ash-veneered 18mm MDF

- Solid ash for lippings and legs

- Ash-veneered 6mm MDF

- Veneer edging tape

- Medium and fine abrasives

- Clear aerosol lacquer

- 3 x pairs easy drawer runners 13 13/16in (350mm) long

- Long drawer handles

- 6mm straight cutter

- Rebate cutter

DIMENSIONAL DIAGRAM

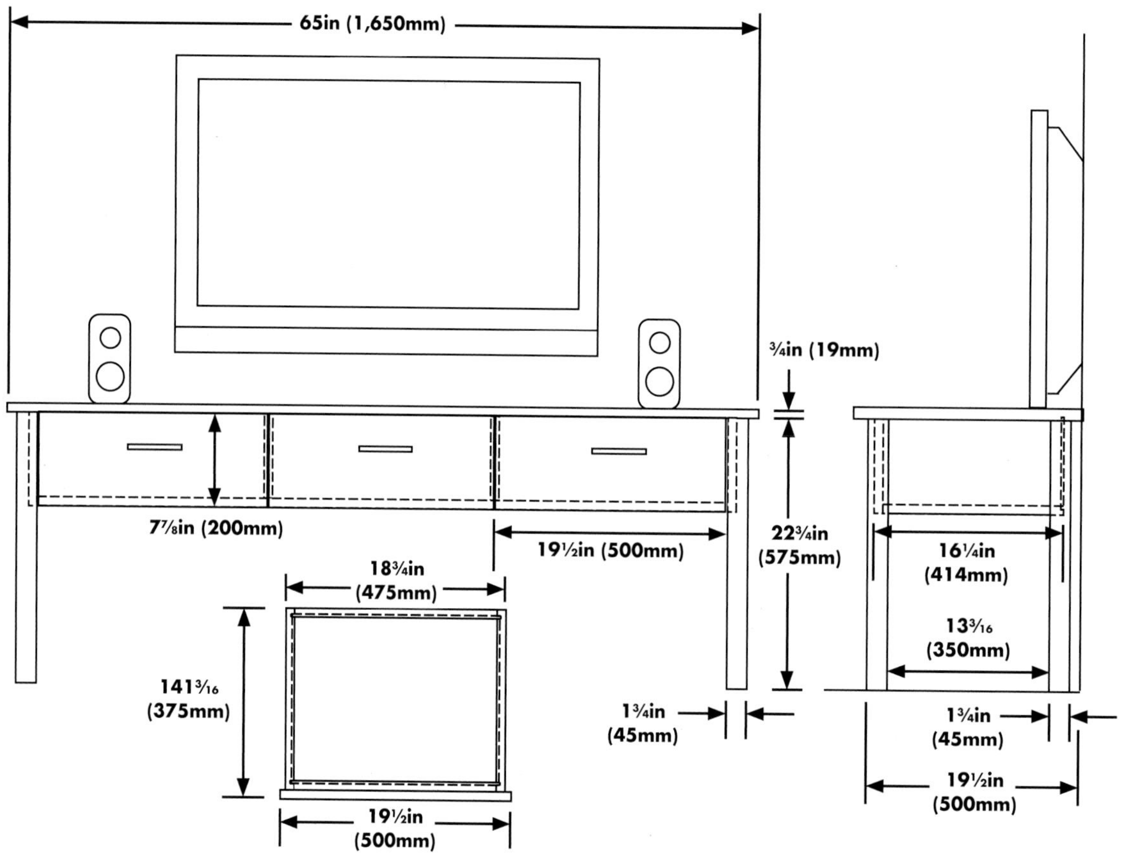

◆ CUTTING LIST

Carcass:

Solid ash lipping ¾ x ¾in (19 x 19mm) sufficient for front and ends of carcass top

Solid ash legs 22 11/16 x 1¾ x 1¾in (575 x 45 x 45mm) x 4

18mm veneered MDF:
Top 63⅜ x 19in (1,610 x 480mm) x 1

Base 59¼ x 15½in (1,516 x 393mm) x 1

Ends 13 3/16 x 7⅞in (350 x 200mm) x 2

Dividers 15 3/16 x 7⅛in (385 x 180mm) x 3

6mm veneered MDF:
Back panel Approx. 60⅜ x 7⅞in (1534 x 198mm) (divided into 3)

Drawer boxes:

18mm veneered MDF:
Front and back Approx. 17⅞ x 5 15/16in (453 x 150mm) x 6

Sides 14 13/16 x 5 15/16in (375 x 150mm) x 6

6mm veneered MDF:
Drawer bottom Approx. 17 11/16 x 13 13/16in (448 x 349mm) x 6

1 Make a cutting list based on the drawings and cut out all the carcass parts. Set the blade so it doesn't protrude far through the veneered board as it will reduce breakout of the veneer surface and cut slightly oversize.

2 Use a large router and straight cutter to trim all edges neatly. Check for square before making each cut.

3 Apply solid lippings to the edges of the unit top. They should be the same thickness as the veneered boards or a fraction thicker, certainly not less.

4 Narrow pieces such as the ends of the unit are better cut on a table saw if you have access to one.

5 Begin marking out the positions of all components on the underside of the top. This in effect becomes a 'rod' or template that tells you exactly where everything will go.

6 The large bottom panel needs to have markings on it taken directly from the top so there is no chance of measuring errors.

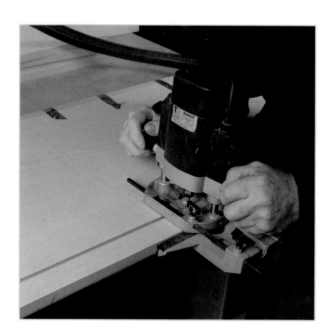

7 The top overhangs all round so the back panel groove being machined here is set some distance in from the back edge.

8 A groove is needed at each end, ready to take the end panels.

9 The bottom panels require rebate rather than a groove. To achieve the correct rebate width you may need to do a bearing swap, as I did here.

10 Machining the bottom panel rebate. Rebating can produce uncollected dust, so wear a mask.

11 The construction relies on loose tongues that are glued into slots in the carcass parts. The slots are just over ¼in (6.4mm) wide, so a ¼in (6mm) ply tongue with glue is sufficient to fill the gap. Take care when cutting these on the table saw; use a sub bed to close the gap around the blade so these narrow components don't get trapped beside the blade.

12 Slotting the ends of boards is a bit of a problem, which is overcome by making up a simple 90° L-jig.

13 Clamp a board in the vice alongside the L-jig and check it is flush from end to end with the top of the jig. It goes without saying that the edges need to be flat and square so all meeting faces do so properly. It can help to align the workpiece to the L-jig by clamping both together before inserting in the vice, then removing the clamps if they foul the router fence.

14 Now fit the fence to the router and centre it on the board edge and proceed to slot it. To avoid the router wandering off course it should normally be pulled towards the operator; if you push, it invariably moves outwards away from the jig.

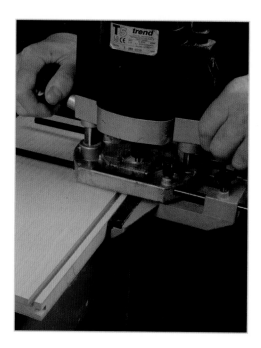

15 The outer ends of the unit need slots, as seen here, because the bottom panel will fit against them again using loose tongues.

16 The legs need to be planed square and also need tongue slots; this is easy if you have two fences to prevent the router from wandering.

17 The finished legs are 'handed'; that is, two go at the left-hand end of an end panel and two to the right. The legs should have been marked up before machining so you don't get a mix up, as this can happen easily.

18 Gluing up an end as a sub assembly. It is only possible to assemble this unit by doing the ends first and leaving them to dry.

19 Clamp the ends together carefully, making sure the legs are not twisted from side to side as this will prevent the carcass from going together correctly.

20 Sand all internal surfaces before assembly. This is good practice as it is difficult to do this properly after assembly.

21 Use a bevel cutter to add a small bevel detail on both the top and bottom edges. A tiny bevel looks right on oak rather than a roundover; however, it isn't needed at the top of the legs where they meet the carcass.

22 Before final assembly, slot in the ends of the bottom panel. This is the same as for the intermediate panels except I found myself higher off the ground using a pair of steps.

★ **WORKING TIP**

There are 'Working At Height' regulations governing trade use of steps and ladders which don't apply to home users, but nevertheless we should all take care working off the ground. Steps and ladders should not only be strong enough but shouldn't wobble; if they do there may be some defect and for the cost it is better to replace them. The type with an extended platform to rest against or hold paint tins is safer to use especially if you are routing above bench height.

23 The leg ends need to be bevelled so they move smoothly on flooring if shifted around. Note how the tough oak end grain has caused burning; a second lighter pass will remove this cleanly.

24 Detail of the meeting slots in the carcass ends. The carcass end is loose tongued to the leg and the lower slot will take the bottom panel while the leg slot will accept the carcass back panel.

25 This is not a time to be interrupted unless someone offers to help hold the unit together while you assemble it. Do a dry run first though and check squareness – better to discover any laying out and machining faults before everything is covered in runny glue!

26 Push the loose tongues into the glue so they sit properly in the grooves. The loose tongues need to be a good fit rather than relying on the glue to fill any gaps. The tongue width should be a millimetre or two less than the two combined slot depths or the joints will not close.

27 Plenty of clamps are needed to pull the whole unit together. It must be checked carefully for squareness everywhere. Note how short clamps have been put together on top to extend them effectively.

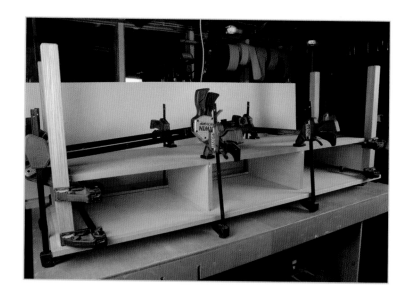

28 The MDF back panel is inserted in sections using a small piece to protect them while tapping them into place. This operation is quite critical because the sectioned back panels will hold the carcass square.

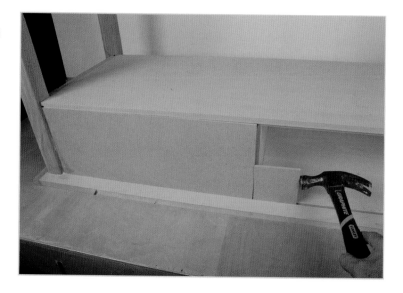

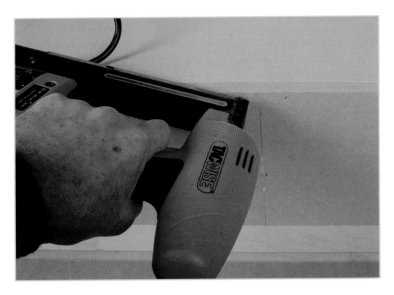

29 The back panel is glued and pinned in place with the joins coinciding with the drawer dividers. Be careful where the back panel joints occur, so that any fixings go into the rear of the divider, or they may show sticking out inside. It can help to aim the pins or pin gun at a slight angle to avoid the problem.

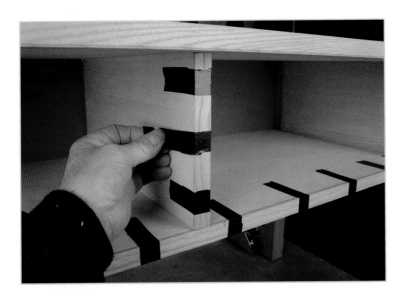

30 The edges of the dividers and the bottom panel now have a solid lipping several millimetres thick glued onto them.

31 You need to work out the drawer dimensions accurately. Measure each space they fit into, as there will be slight differences. Using easy runners, you need to allow ½in (12.5mm) per side gap. The drawer needs to stop short of the carcass back and you need a gap above so each drawer can be hooked into its runners. The drawer box front and back will fit inside the sides of the drawer and a ¼in (6mm) panel is grooved into the drawer bottom.

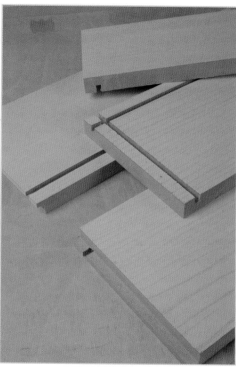

32 Make the grooves in the sides to take the front and back components. Keep the board pressed against the fence all through the cut so the groove doesn't deviate and weaken the resultant joints.

33 The drawer bottom grooves are made in the same way. The drawer front and back have tongues cut with a rebate cutter so they can fit into the sides.

34 Iron-on edging is used to finish the top edges; the excess will be trimmed off. Some stockists will sell you edging tape by the metre; it is not so cheap per metre but will cost less overall as you do not need lots of it.

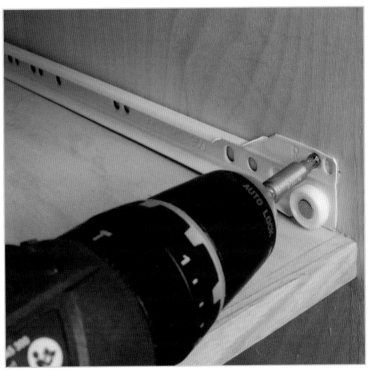

35 Use a sharp chisel very carefully to take away the overhanging veneer. The edges will need a light sanding. You can buy special edging tape trimmers but a sharp broad chisel running flat against the board side in order to get a neat finish works. However, do respect the grain of the veneer or it may tear out.

36 The easy runners in position and the drawer front with handle fitted. The separate front may need some adjustment to get the fit correct with just a ⅛in (2mm) gap all round. It is screwed to the drawer box from the inside.

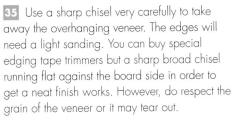

★ WORKING TIP

Modern 'easy-on' drawer runners are not difficult to fit. However, make sure you have got the drawer width right or they may not fit along the sides. They fit just inside the carcass nearly resting on the base. The screws to fix them are not long but the heads need to be small enough so they don't interfere with the sliding action. The other half of the drawer components screw in from underneath the drawer box. Once installed the drawer box then hooks into the receiving part of the runners in the carcass. For that reason the drawer box needs clearance above it inside the carcass.

The finished flat-screen media centre.

ROOM SKIRTING AND ARCHITRAVE

Everyone has painted softwood architrave and skirtings in their house, but what if you want something different? Say, oak or mahogany? Why not? Cost is an issue, but you cannot usually buy it off the shelf. However, with a large router and a router table you can make your own without much difficulty. The trick is to use veneered MDF for all large flat sections and add moulded solid timber afterwards. This keeps the cost down and makes everything easier to handle when machining. A good timber yard will not only sell you veneered board but will cut it to suitable widths for a charge.

MATERIALS AND TOOLS

- Prepared hardwood sections suitable for moulding

- Veneered MDF board cut into strips (sized to suit room proportions)

- Medium and fine abrasives

- Satin or gloss wood finishes

- Builders' mastic

- Long screws and wall plugs

- Skirting and/or other suitable moulding cutters

- Plug cutter

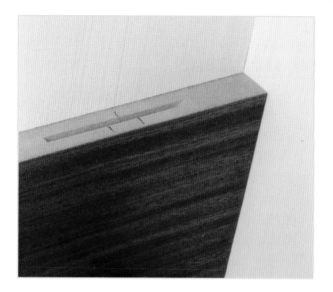

1 First cut the flat sections to fit the walls. Walls in older properties are seldom square or flat, so you need to allow for that. Internal corners only need boards butted up against each other. The outer corner will be mitred carefully so the cuts meet properly. A pullover mitre saw is the best way to do this neatly and quickly. Be careful to check for the presence of cables or pipework.

2 The door lining is also veneered board. It needs to stand slightly proud of the wall surfaces so the architrave will lie flat on it when fixed in place. The door-stop section has also been added. Keep your fixings as neat as possible – no hammer work allowed! Instead drill countersinks and plug over-long screws that run into wallplugs that are fitted into pre-drilled holes unless you are just fixing into studwork.

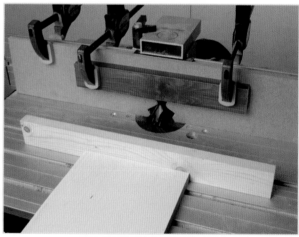

3 There are a number of cutters available for machining architrave and skirting top. Here from left to right are: Grecian ogee, Modern Torus, Victorian torus. The Grecian ogee is available in large and small sizes.

4 The sections you are going to mould must be machined to the same section and square. This needs to be done on a planer thicknesser, although some timber yards supply it ready prepared. Here, a Grecian ogee cutter is fitted in the table, with a breakthrough fence and batten acting as a hold-down and a support on the left that will press the timber against the fence.

5 The first pass should not remove a lot of timber so you can see how well the set-up is coping with the cut. Note how the supports are holding the timber in place but also surrounding it like a tunnel, giving the operator protection and eliminating vibration for a much smoother result.

6 Here are the stages of cut as the wood is gradually removed. The last cut is set so the round nose or sweep of the moulding is still left with the wood at full width at that level. The thin cove near the top is okay because the wood will still remain intact once it is fixed to the wall.

7 This skirting section near the door frame needs to be marked and cut so it will butt up to the architrave. Note the biscuit slots in the top and also visible in the first photo. Do this before fitting the skirting so the top section can also be slotted and fitted on afterwards with glue.

8 This unsealed section of architrave is tested to check it will fit properly. Apart from a few pins to hold it to the door lining, builders' mastic is the strong, discreet way to fix decorative architrave and skirting top in place without marring it with screws or nails.

9 Here, mastic is used alone to give a very strong bond to the wall without screws or nails.

10 Glue and size 20 biscuits are used to secure the skirting top permanently. Note that the moulding is mitred, whereas the flat boards are simply butted together.

11 The job complete, a folded piece of abrasive paper is used to lift the right-hand section level until the mastic has set.

12 If you want to go further and add more mouldings to the room walls, you can start by making a dado moulding, which runs approximately two fifths of room height up the wall. Here, a section is being moulded with side and top pressure supports to hold it safely while it is being fed over the cutter.

13 This multi-form cutter has been used to produce a wall frame moulding on the left and dado rail on the right. You can do this by raising or lowering the cutter and choosing to lay the workpiece flat or standing it up when machining.

★ WORKING TIP

In this example the door lining part has been screwed into the adjoining studwork and the screw holes plugged, while the skirting has been bonded to the wall using builders' mastic, which is an easy modern solution. However, it is often better to use a masonry drill and wallplugs with screws for a more satisfactory fixing. You do need to be sure, however, that there are no pipes or wires lurking beneath the wall surface. You can use a pipe and wire detector as a guide, but study where sockets and radiators are as well because this can also give you a good indication.

The finished room skirting and architrave.

14 A careful blend of well-proportioned woodwork, paint and wallpaper can create a very smart traditional look to a room. The mouldings can be painted softwood or hardwood such as this utile timber, which looks much like mahogany.

SET OF DRAWERS

This small set of drawers would look good in the bathroom, kitchen, bedroom or lounge depending on how you finish it and your choice of colour. There is more to making the set of drawers than might appear: this is a good exercise in orderly and accurate parts preparation and basic table-machining technique. It also proves my belief that the most useful cutters you can own are straight cutters – in this case quite a small one for machining all the grooves. I used MDF for the carcass as I wanted to paint that. The drawers are made from birch ply, which is easy and pleasant to machine and has a quite subtle grain pattern that I brought out by finishing with clear aerosol lacquer. There are plenty of small knobs to choose from, but I went for chrome as it lightened the look of the piece.

● MATERIALS AND TOOLS

- Offcuts of 9mm birch ply
- Offcuts of 9mm MDF
- Piece of 3.2mm hardboard

- PVA glue
- Try square

- 3.2mm straight cutter
- Small rebate cutter

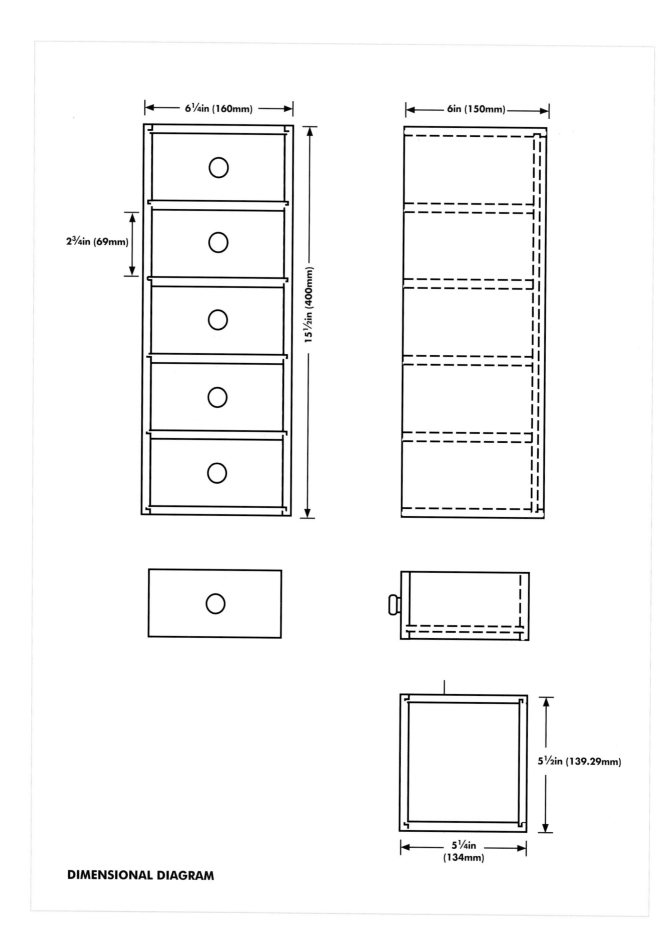

DIMENSIONAL DIAGRAM

◆ CUTTING LIST

MDF carcass:

Sides 15¾ x 5 15/16 x ⅜in (400 x 150 x 9mm) x 2

Drawer dividers, top and bottom 6 1/16 x 5 7/16 x ⅜in (154 x 137 x 9mm) x 6

Back panel 15 5/16 x 6 1/16 x ¼in (388 x 154 x 6mm) x 1

(Carcass openings to be checked before making drawers)

Birch ply drawers:

Front 5½ x 2⅝ x ⅜in (140 x 67 x 9mm) x 5

Back
5⅛ x 2⅝ x ⅜in (130 x 67 x 9mm) x 5

Sides 5 1/16 x 2⅝ x ⅜in (126 x 67 x 9mm) x 5

Base 4⅞ x 5⅛ x ⅛in (123 x 130 x 3.2mm) x 5

1 Cut out the carcass parts excluding the back panel, which will be cut to fit later. Take the two sides and mark all the drawer dividers across both components so they match. The construction is tongue and groove, so you need to mark the tongue positions too. All of the tongues will be at the top of each divider as you view the drawer carcass when it is standing up. The exception is the top one: this must have its tongue on the underside, otherwise the joint will become an unintentional rebate, which is far weaker.

2 Machine all the grooves in carcass sides using edge marks for guidance. Do one half, then spin it round to make the two grooves at the other end. Do not forget the position of the topmost slot is different; thus the fence must be adjusted slightly to suit. A ⅛in (3.2mm) straight cutter was chosen for this work.

3 All the grooves are now correctly cut. The dividers need to have a rebate machined at each end so they are a good tight fit in the grooves. Note that the four middle dividers are not so deep because a back panel will be fitted behind them. Make sure you cut all like components at the same time so they match, and have an extra one or two blanks in case you need to get a better fit. Do not keep testing the joints repeatedly as the MDF will start to break up and loosen them.

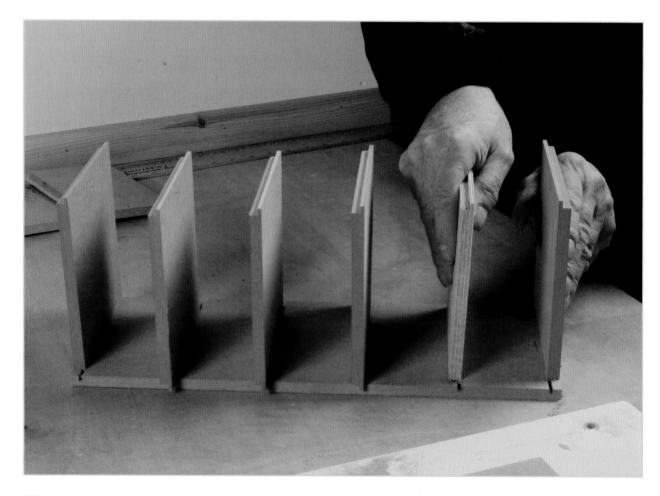

4 Check the dividers all sit in their grooves nicely and the drawer spacings are correct. Machine a groove along one long edge of the sides and matching grooves in the top and bottom dividers to take a thin ply back panel.

5 The carcass has its back panel cut to size and inserted in the grooves at the rear of the carcass, which is now glued and clamped. Check the carcass is square and wipe away any surplus glue.

6 Cut sufficient strips of birch ply for the drawers and check they fit in the openings. You may need to allocate specific strips to each opening if there are minor size differences. Have some spare material because these drawers use more than you might imagine. Keep each set of drawer components together and mark which position they will fit in.

7 Once again, the construction is with tongue and groove with the bottom panels let into a groove all round the inside at the base. The components are quite narrow; I opted to use a through fence so they would run smoothly over the cutter. You can also help this operation by using a square push-block.

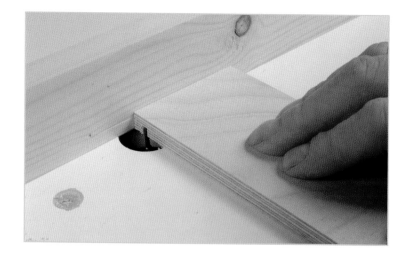

8 Here are the components for one drawer laid out to show the grooves required. The sides and the back panel will now need a rebate to form the tongues.

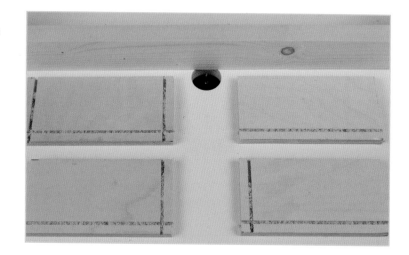

9 The tongue is being formed on a drawer side. The convention for drawers with an integral front panel is that the front panel covers the sides that are jointed into it, whereas the sides fit over the ends of the back panel, which is stronger and ensures that the drawer sides slide easily inside the carcass.

11 Cut the drawer bases to size and glue and assemble each drawer. Clamp up and once the glue is dry, check the fit and if necessary number the drawers underneath so you know where each one fits best. Break the arrises (edges) with abrasive spraymounted to a piece of ply so there are no sharp or ragged edges.

■ CHOOSING HARDWARE

This is a fun bit, locating and choosing suitable hardware. You can buy online but I don't recommend it as you need to check your choice against an actual drawer. Although the finish, whether bright brass, antiqued (patinated), chrome, porcelain or even plastic, is important, size also matters. Too small and you cannot grip the knob, too large and it will look ugly and out of proportion. Try and find a hardware dealer you can visit and take one drawer along with you. They should be perfectly happy for you to go through their stock to make the right choice.

10 Check the fit of each drawer before gluing them together. If they are tight from side to side you can trim the back panel a fraction and rerun the rebate cut so the drawer will slide in properly.

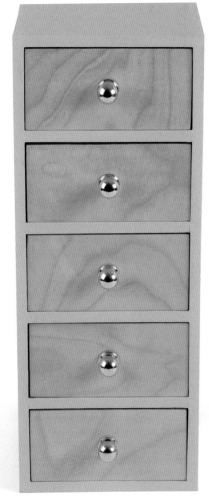

The finished set of drawers.

KITCHEN TOWEL HOLDER

Here is a neat way to keep your kitchen towel available but still fitting in with kitchen surroundings. It doesn't require much wood, only a certain amount of ingenuity in machining it. The result is quite pleasing.

● MATERIALS AND TOOLS

- Pine offcuts

- Medium abrasive paper

- PVA glue

- Water-based lacquer

- 28mm or similar size forstner bit

- Small V-point cutter

- 12.7mm roundover cutter

- 6.4mm roundover cutter

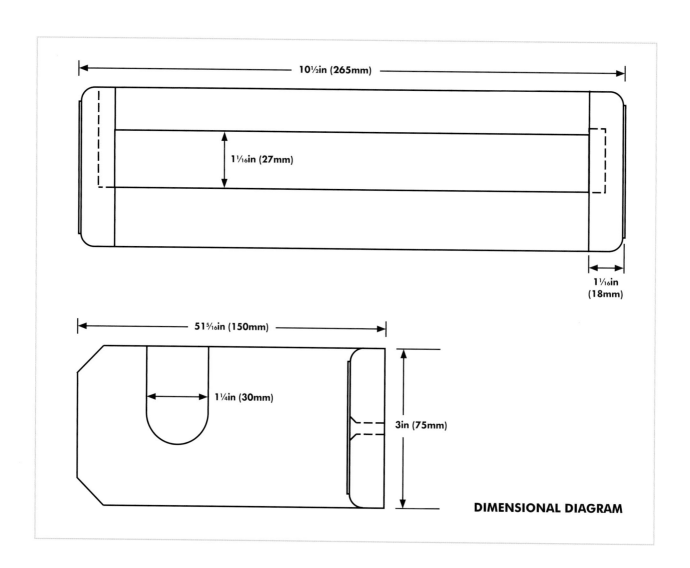

10½in (265mm)

1¹⁄₁₆in (27mm)

1¹⁄₁₆in (18mm)

5⁵⁄₁₆in (150mm)

1¼in (30mm)

3in (75mm)

DIMENSIONAL DIAGRAM

1 We first need a special jig in order to make dowel to put the kitchen roll on. It needs to match the rest of the holder, hence the need to make a jig. First cut a strip of board and drill and countersink down one side to take screws.

2 Fix one batten in place with another one loose underneath to level it while screwdriving.

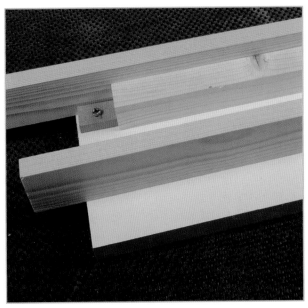

3 Take a square section of your chosen wood – in this case, pine. This is cut overlength and held in the jig with two small pads of MDF and screws.

4 Fix the other batten in place; both will support a router sitting on top and a large roundover cutter that needs to be clear of the workpiece and batten.

5 The workpiece is about 1in (25mm) square; therefore the rounder radius needs to be half that at 12.7mm – the standard UK cutter. Fit it in the router and plunge the static router so the roundover neatly touches on the top of the workpiece at the outer wing of the cutter. Keep it away from the sides, switch on and press against the workpiece, and machine into the cutter path, moving from left to right.

6 Once the first radius is complete, turn the wood over 90° and machine the next curve, and so on. As it loses its corners, the workpiece will need to be pressed against the jig, keeping fingers clear of the cutter.

7 The finished section is surprisingly round in section. A little sanding is needed to remove any ridging and it is ready for use.

8 Mark out the holder ends with the middle in between and leaving a waste area in between to allow for any trimming. The waste areas are pencilled out, and the recess to hold the dowel is marked. At the other end it is just a circular recess. The slot allows the roll to be changed.

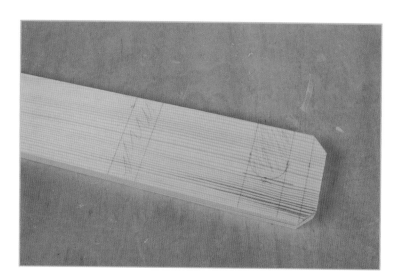

9 Here the slot detail is more visible. It doesn't go down very far – the large cardboard tube in the kitchen roll will make it hang low in any case, so it looks better with the dowel higher.

10 Use a forstner drill (not a spade bit) to drill the initial hole at each end. At the slot end the holes are drilled overlapping to create the slot. The forstner cuts cleanly without a long protruding centre marking the wood.

11 Using a sharp chisel, clean the sides and the bottom of the slotted end to a smooth finish.

12 Mark the centre section for drilling wall-fixing holes. This is done from the reverse side, because, as will become apparent later, the decorative moulding is done on this side too. The ends have been carefully cut and the edges sanded.

13 Use a small V-point cutter to drill the fixing holes. The router will slip around while drilling; to counteract this, use spray adhesive to stick two pieces of medium abrasive on the router baseplate. Stand the router upright and trim off the surplus abrasive paper with a knife on the backing paper side.

14 Aim the cutter carefully on the cross lines and plunge enough to allow the screw head to sink in and to fit a matching wood plug on top. Run a drill through the centre for the screw shank.

15 Fit a 6.4mm roundover cutter in the table and raise it enough to create a slight step on the front of the workpiece. The bearing must run against the side and not slip into the slot above; it will ruin the cut if it does so.

16 Move the workpiece against the cutter and machine all round including the ends. Do this in a smooth continuous motion to avoid burning, which usually occurs when the wood is moving very slowly or standing still.

17 Cut the three components apart on the marked pencil lines. They need to be slotted to take biscuits so they can be joined together. A biscuit jointer is the safest and most accurate way to do this. Note that the back piece has its moulding on the front, of course, while the ends have their mouldings on the outside of the holder.

18 Sand all components smooth, taking care to remove all pencil marks. Use hand abrasive to sand the edges.

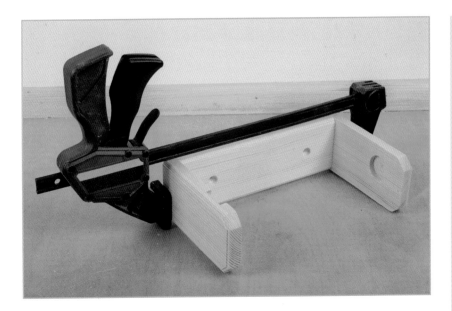

19 Glue and biscuit the holder together and clamp carefully. Make sure the ends are perpendicular to the back piece. If not, adjust the clamp position until they are.

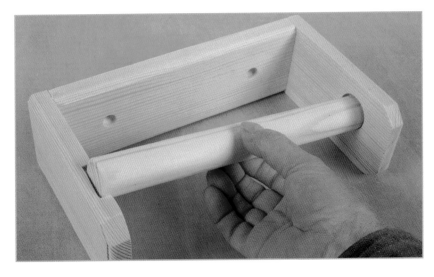

20 Cut the dowel slightly under length and round the ends with abrasive paper. Use water-based lacquer to seal the wood and avoid it getting grubby. Check that the dowel fits before fixing the kitchen towel holder to the wall.

★ **WORKING TIP**

Squaring up assembled components can be easy to overlook. In the case of the kitchen towel holder this is very true. I use a lot of modern 'quick clamps' often in preference to older-style metal sash clamps. They work very well but it is very easy to get something out of square and not realise it.

The first thing is to sight by eye; if it looks wrong it probably is. Check internal or external angles with an accurate square. Now loosen the offending clamp and adjust the position of the clamp faces enough to make a difference. Experience will show which direction you need to move the faces for a given result. Do not apply too much pressure as it can bow components and suggests the joint wasn't well made in the first place.

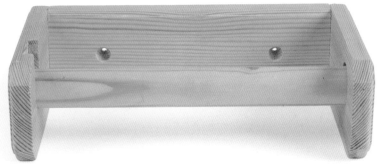

The finished kitchen towel holder.

CIRCULAR MIRROR FRAME

Here is a good excuse to use a router trammel to great effect. Quite quickly and simply, a beautiful-looking mirror frame can be created. Once mouldings are added all round and paint applied, no one would know there was just a plain piece of MDF underneath!

● MATERIALS AND TOOLS

- A board offcut of 15mm MDF larger than 21½in (545mm) square

- Medium abrasive paper

- Paint

- Gilt paste

- Router trammel

- Small rebate cutter

- Small ovolo cutter

- Small classical cutter

DIMENSIONAL DIAGRAM

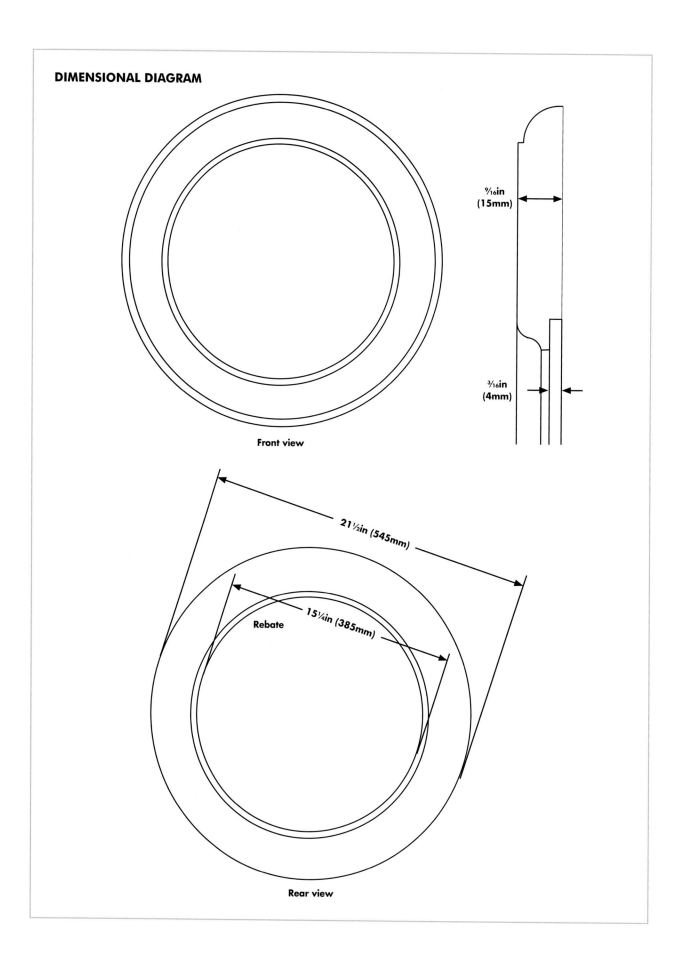

%₁₆in
(15mm)

³⁄₁₆in
(4mm)

Front view

21½in (545mm)

15¼in (385mm)

Rebate

Rear view

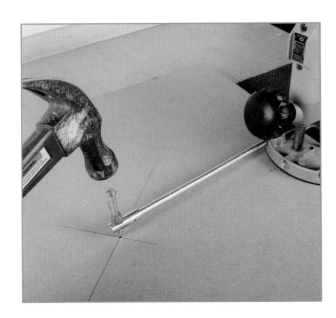

1 Choose a suitable size mirror either with or without pre-drilled holes for wall fixing. If you cannot get one without holes or you want a specific size, a glass merchant should be able to cut one to your requirements.

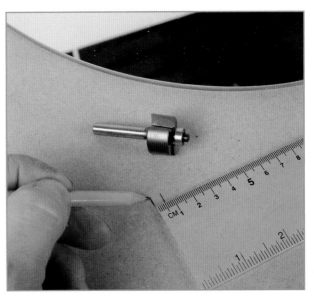

2 Work out the size of rebate your cutter will produce and the offset required for machining the mirror hole in a piece of MDF. You will need to leave a gap all round the mirror in the rebate of 1mm, so the mirror will sit in neatly.

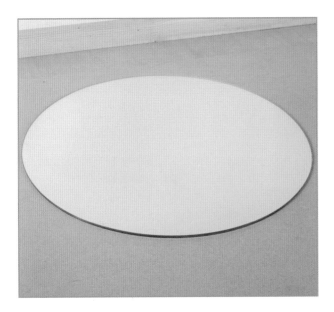

3 Mark the centre of the board and set the trammel for the outside cut, first using a hammer to tap the point into the board.

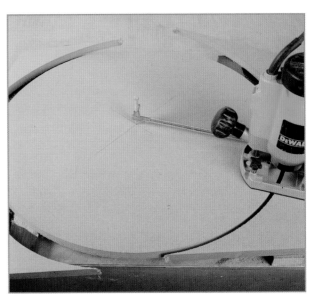

4 Machine the outside away in a number of passes to final depth. Use extraction, as a lot of dust will be produced.

5 Now machine the inside curve having carefully set the trammel to the size worked out earlier. The centre will drop away when you break through.

6 Set the rebate cutter up in the table and adjust the cutter against the mirror so you make the rebate deep enough.

7 Place the frame on the table, switch the router on and machine into the rotation of the cutter, moving smoothly all the way around. Perform this operation again just to be sure it is completely even so the mirror will sit flat. Note the extraction pipe.

8 The mirror fits perfectly with just a slight gap, as expected.

9 A small classical pattern cutter is used to relieve and detail the inner front edge of the frame.

10 A roundover cutter is used to mould the outer edge leaving a deliberate step profile.

★ **WORKING TIP**

Although you need a moulding at the front of a mirror frame or photo frame and a glass and picture rebate at the rear, it does carry a risk. You need to ensure there is still enough 'land' between the two for the bearing to run against. Check this at the outset before you start a project and, if necessary, use thicker material to avoid this problem. MDF comes in 3mm thickness variations, i.e. 6, 9, 12, 15 and 18mm, so you can find something to suit the job.

11 You can paint the frame any colour you want; I used satin black and then rubbed gilt paste into the mouldings for an interesting effect.

The finished circular mirror frame.

GLOSSARY

Aliphatic resin glue
A glue with a high tack rate for rapid initial bonding.

Arbor
A shank on which cutters, bearings and spacers can be fitted.

Architrave
Moulding applied around a doorway.

Astragal
A small semicircular moulding on a flat strip, often used as a cabinet glazing bar.

Backfeeding
Deliberately pushing work the wrong way on a router table. This is a dangerous practice with a few specific exceptions.

Bead
A half-round shape.

Bolection
A moulding that projects beyond the frame to which it is applied.

Breakout (or tearout)
Torn wood fibres, especially across the grain.

Brushes
Graphite carbon blocks that transmit electricity to a rotating commutator.

Bullnose
A traditional moulding profile.

Cabinetmaking
The construction of furniture.

Carpentry
Applying sawn and prepared timber to buildings.

Cavetto
A cove shape with a small shoulder at each end.

Classical
A common term for a moulding that has a cove and roundover with a step in between.

Collet
A split metal sleeve that grips onto the cutter shank.

Commutator
The sectioned collar on the motor spindle to which each winding is separately connected.

Cornice
A moulding that overhangs the top of a piece of furniture.

Dado
A moulding fixed low down to protect a wall from furniture and to mark a break in decor.

Depth turret
A rotating casting on the router base. It has adjustable points so that different plunge depths can be set.

Door lining
The wooden frame in a doorway on which the door is hung.

Door stop
The small strip of wood against which the door shuts.

Drop box
A container situated between the router and the extractor that collects heavy chippings.

Face and edge (UK)
A term denoting the two best adjoining surfaces on prepared wood, marked by a pencil.

Face moulding
A moulding cut into the front surface of the wood.

Fine adjuster
A means of altering the cutter height with great precision.

Fixed-head router
An overhead-mounted machine. The work moves underneath it.

Fixed pilot/guide pin
A round section at the end of a cutter to guide it. Inferior to bearings.

Glazing bar
A wooden bar that separates each pane of glass.

Grain
The general direction or arrangement of the fibres in wood.

Guide bearing
An enclosed ball-bearing race of an exact size. It allows the cutter to follow a shape accurately.

Guide bush
A simple metal collar that keeps the cutter a set distance from the workpiece.

HP or Horsepower
Measure of energy produced at the router spindle or shaft.

HPLV
High pressure, low volume. Small vacuum-cleaner-type extractor.

HSE
Health and Safety Executive. In the UK, an agency responsible for safety in the workplace.

HSS (high-speed steel)
An alloy of steel, superior to plain carbon steel, which is used for machining applications.

HVLP
High volume, low pressure. A large industrial extraction machine.

Joinery (UK)
Making wood components, such as windows and doors, that are fitted into buildings.

Joinery (US)
Making all furniture and fittings.

Lamb's tongue
An aptly named traditional moulding profile.

Lead-in point
A shaped finger of wood that gives support to curved workpieces.

MDF
Medium density fibreboard. Made with compressed wood fibre and resin.

Micron
A unit of measure used to describe small particles, especially dust from wood.

Motor winding
One of a series of varnished copper electrical wires spun around a central steel core.

Ogee
A classical moulding consisting of a concave and a convex form.

PAR
'Prepared all round'. Timber that is planed on all four surfaces.

Per cube foot (UK)
How hardwoods are sold in the UK.

Per metre run (UK)
How softwood is sold in the UK.

Picture rail
A revived moulding, placed high up on the wall and used to hang picture frames.

Planted moulding
A moulding applied to existing woodwork.

Polyurethane glue
A glue that foams slightly on application. It sets quickly and can be used on wet wood.

Pre-scoring
A very shallow preliminary cut slicing the wood fibres, thus preventing tearout when deep cutting.

PVA
Polyvinyl acetate. A cheap and reliable glue for ordinary use.

Rising cutter
When a heavy cut causes a cutter to slide out of a worn collet.

Roller guide
A device to make a router follow irregular shapes.

Roller stands
Supports for wood as it enters and leaves a machine table.

Sawn timber
Timber that has been cut into usable sections, but requires proper planing before it can be used.

Sealed bearings

These are superior to ordinary ballraces. They are designed for high-speed work and keep out dust.

Shank

A precision-machined plain section on the cutter that slides into the collet.

Shaw guard

A type of combined hold-down and guard for safe working on woodworking machines.

Skirting

A large, moulded strip to decorate and finish a wall where it meets the floor.

Skis

Metal strips that support the router above the work so it can move over uneven areas.

Sprung fingers

A hold-down that uses thin fingers or tines to press wood against the fence.

Superglue

An adhesive containing cyanoacrylate that is useful for instant minor wood repairs.

TCT (tungsten-carbide-tipped)

A type of cutter. Tungsten carbide is a metal alloy used for cutting abrasive materials.

Through fence

A wooden facing completely covering the cutter gap in the existing table fences.

Timber (lumber in the US)

Felled trees, partly converted or unconverted for use.

Torus top

A skirting top moulding featuring a half-round shape.

Trammel

A point and arm for drawing or cutting large circles.

Tufnol

Industrial sheet material suitable for jigmaking and so on.

Twinfast

A type of modern screw with a parallel shank and two driving threads.

Urea formaldehyde glue

An adhesive that sets hard and is good for filling gaps.

Veneer A wafer-thin sheet of wood (usually about 0.6mm thick) glued to a board.

Veneer pins Tiny pins, thinner than panel pins, that are useful for neat, split-free fixings.

Watts

Expression of a router's electrical consumption and output.

CONVERSION CHART

Imperial to metric						Metric to imperial	
Inches (fractions)	Inches (decimal)	Millimetres	Inches (fractions)	Inches (decimal)	Millimetres	Millimetres	Inches
1/64	0.0156	0.3969	33/64	0.5156	13.0969	1	0.0394
1/32	0.0313	0.7938	17/32	0.5313	13.4938	1.5	0.0591
3/64	0.0469	1.1906	35/64	0.5469	13.8906	2	0.0787
1/16	0.0625	1.5875	9/16	0.5625	14.2875	2.5	0.0984
5/64	0.0781	1.9844	37/64	0.5781	14.6844	3	0.1181
3/32	0.0938	2.3813	19/32	0.5938	15.0813	3.5	0.1378
7/64	0.1094	2.7781	39/64	0.6094	15.4781	4	0.1575
1/8	0.1250	3.1750	5/8	0.6250	15.8750	4.5	0.1772
9/64	0.1406	3.5719	41/64	0.6406	16.2719	5	0.1969
5/32	0.1563	3.9688	21/32	0.6563	16.6688	5.5	0.2165
11/64	0.1719	4.3656	43/64	0.6719	17.0656	6	0.2362
3/16	0.1875	4.7625	11/16	0.6875	17.4625	6.5	0.2559
13/64	0.2031	5.1594	45/64	0.7031	17.8594	7	0.2756
7/32	0.2188	5.5563	23/32	0.7188	18.2563	7.5	0.2953
15/64	0.2344	5.9531	47/64	0.7344	18.6531	8	0.3150
1/4	0.2500	6.3500	3/4	0.7500	19.0500	8.5	0.3346
17/64	0.2656	6.7469	49/64	0.7656	19.4469	9	0.3543
7/32	0.2813	7.1438	25/32	0.7813	19.8438	9.5	0.3740
19/64	0.2969	7.5406	51/64	0.7969	20.2406	10	0.3937
5/16	0.3125	7.9375	13/16	0.8125	20.6375	10.5	0.4134
21/64	0.3281	8.3344	53/64	0.8281	21.0344	11	0.4331
11/32	0.3438	8.7313	27/32	0.8438	21.4313	11.5	0.4528
23/64	0.3594	9.1281	55/64	0.8594	21.8281	12	0.4724
3/8	0.3750	9.5250	7/8	0.8750	22.2250	12.5	0.4921
25/64	0.3906	9.9219	57/64	0.8906	22.6219	13	0.5118
13/32	0.4063	10.3188	29/32	0.9063	23.0188	13.5	0.5315
27/64	0.4219	10.7156	59/64	0.9219	23.4156	14	0.5512
7/16	0.4375	11.1125	15/16	0.9375	23.8125	14.5	0.5709
29/64	0.4531	11.5094	61/64	0.9531	24.2094	15	0.5906
15/32	0.4688	11.9063	31/32	0.9688	24.6063	15.5	0.6102
31/64	0.4844	12.3031	63/64	0.9844	25.0031	16	0.6299
1/2	0.5000	12.7000	1	1.0000	25.4000	16.5	0.6496

SUPPLIERS

USA

Bosch
www.boschtools.com

Power tool manufacturer

DeWalt
www.dewalt.com

Power tool manufacturer

Freud
www.freudtools.com

Manufacturer of router bits and tooling

Kreg
www.kregtool.com

Manufacturer of precision routing systems

Lee Valley
www.leevalley.com/us

Supplier of a wide range of hand and power tools
and router accessories

MLCS
www.mlcswoodworking.com

Supplier of router bits, tables and accessories

Porter Cable
www.portercable.com

Power tool manufacturer

Rockler
www.rockler.com

Supplier of woodworking supplies and power tools

Rousseau
www.rousseauco.com

Manufacturer of machine and router accessories and tables

Whiteside
www.whitesiderouterbits.com

Manufacturer of router cutters

UK

General

Axminster Tool Centre
www.axminster.co.uk

Tool dealer for routers, cutters and accessories

Trend Machinery & Cutting Tools Ltd
www.trend-uk.com

Manufacturer of routers, cutters and accessories

Cutters

Wealden Tool Company
www.wealdentool.com

Manufacturers of router cutters

Titman UK
www.titman.co.uk

Manufacturer of router cutters

Whiteside Machine Co.
www.routercutter.co.uk

American manufacturer of router cutters

Rutlands
www.rutlands.co.uk

Supplier of router cutters

Infinity Tools
www.infinitytools.co.uk

American router cutters

Routers

Robert Bosch UK
www.bosch-pt.co.uk/powertools

Trade and DIY rated power tools including routers

Hitachi Power Tools UK
www.hitachi-powertools.co.uk

Professional power tools including routers

DeWalt UK
www.dewalt.co.uk

Trade rated power tools including routers

Makita UK
www.makitauk.com

Trade rated power tools including routers

Metabo UK
www.metabo.co.uk

Trade rated power tools including routers

Draper Tools
www.draper.co.uk

Supplier of own-brand power tools including routers

ABOUT THE AUTHOR

Anthony has had an interest in woodwork ever since his days at Technical High School in North Kent, which was a very long time ago! However, on leaving school he followed his other major interest of photography. Through the kind offices of a family friend, he started on a wage of six pounds a week as a lowly photographic assistant at Carlton Studios near Marble Arch. He remained there until the mid-1980s, becoming a still-life photographer during that time.

Anthony returned to his passion with wood and started a successful antique restoration business, but having met future wife Patsy and with a family on the way, he chose a more secure occupation working as a cabinetmaker for an interior design company. He then struck out as a designer-maker, followed by spells working for a joinery company and a bespoke kitchen company. Having acquired this ecclectic range of skills Anthony was then asked by the late Paul Richardson, then editor of *The Woodworker* magazine, to write for the publication. He went on to join GMC Publications as a staff photographer, following Paul, who worked as the editor of *Furniture & Cabinetmaking* magazine.

Since then, Anthony has had spells as chief photographer and editor of *The Router* magazine and then technical editor of *Woodworking Plans and Projects*, while still performing the role of chief photographer. He later had the word 'technical' removed from his job title and become simply 'editor' – less, of course, meaning more!

You may well ask yourself how Anthony has managed to do all these different jobs without any training whatsoever. Let's just say he's a quick learner and leave it at that, shall we?

Anthony and Patsy and their family live in sight of the South Downs in Sussex in a delightful village setting. The whole family are very creative, but his youngest daughter Amber has chosen to follow in his footsteps by doing a BA in Restoration and Conservation at Buckinghamshire New University, High Wycombe, UK. Anthony is understandably rather envious of such a rich learning experience and wishes he had had the same opportunity. However, it hasn't stopped him being successful in both the woodworking and publishing worlds.

ACKNOWLEDGEMENTS

Ron Fox, who showed me there was a lot more to routing than just pushing the plug in and switching the damned thing on! Mark Baker, for putting up with my petulant behaviour.

Everyone else who knows me, oh, and Virginia, my hardworking Project Editor, for knocking this book back into shape after I had a bit of a go at it...

PICTURE CREDITS

All photographs by the author, except on the following pages: Page 14 Ray McInnis, www.woodworkinghistory. com (bottom) Pages 32–35 as labelled on each page; pages 74–77 as labelled on each page; page 100 Axminster Tools (top left and top middle) Rutlands (top right, bottom left and bottom right), Trend Ltd (bottom middle); page 127 Bob Seymour (bottom); page 128 Axminster Tools (bottom left), Roger Smith (bottom middle and bottom right); page 129 (top) Paul Richardson; page 133 Axminster Tools (top); page 135 Axminster Tools (top); page 136 Trend Ltd (bottom); page 137 Trend Ltd (top and middle); page 139 Rutlands (top), Legacy USA (bottom). Illustration on page 48 by John Yates.

INDEX

To order a book or request a catalogue, contact:

GMC Publications Ltd

Castle Place, 166 High Street, Lewes, East Sussex, BN7 1XU, United Kingdom

Tel: +44 (0)1273 488005   www.gmcbooks.com